THRONE RIGHTS

KEN CHANT

THRONE RIGHTS

KEN CHANT

ISBN 978-1-61529-060-4

Vision Publishing
1672 Main Street E 109
Ramona, CA 92065
1-800-9-VISION
www.booksbyvision.edu

CONTENTS

PREFACE

The basic theme of these chapters is answered prayer. That may seem on the surface to be a simple theme. But having now completed the series I am conscious once again that I have done little more than fumble with the fringes of my subject. The following pages could hardly be considered anything more than a wondering learner's introduction to the exciting matters with which they deal.

Nonetheless, I hope that you will find here much encouragement for your faith, and that the result of your studies will be a richer experience, not just of prayer itself, but of answered prayer. Not all prayer is answered. But the right kind of prayer, prayed by the right person, in the right way, and to the right God, always **is!**

These Chapters are not written in strict sequence, with each idea confined to one section. Instead, they are built around groups of ideas, at times repeated, then looked at from different angles and set within different emphases. The various aspects of successful prayer are so interwoven into each other that this kind of group approach to the subject is virtually inevitable.

On the matter of prayer itself: I am sadly aware that there are many marvellous passages of scripture I have not so much as mentioned, and many others that have received only passing attention. It was simply not possible for me to deal even briefly with many scriptures that actually do deserve extended comment. However, I have tried to cover at least some of the most important general principles of successful prayer, and in particular, throughout the book, to highlight those emphases that reflect a charismatic **approach to prayer.**

There are doubtless many exceptions, but it would be broadly true to say that charismatics do tend to have an approach to prayer rather different from that of the older evangelical school. Prayer in charismatic circles tends to be less agonising and more affirmative, less passive and more aggressive, less concerned with penitence and more eager to assert authority.

That comment is not meant to disparage the manner of prayer employed by other Christians, but simply to emphasise that we are privileged to be alive at a time when the Holy Spirit is calling the church world-wide to reach a level of achievement in prayer beyond anything it has ever known in its history. The Psalmist spoke truly when he declared that all flesh would hasten to worship the God who answers prayer (65:2). The greatest revival the world has ever seen would break loose if the widespread failure of the church to enjoy answered prayer could be turned into widespread success.

Let us then together echo the cry of the disciples, "*Lord, teach us to pray!*" (Lu 11:1). And let us then be ready to be taught by the Lord, and so to begin praying in a way that will release the Holy Spirit to fulfil scripture in us, and to "*do exceedingly abundantly above all that we can ask or even think!*" (Ep 3:20)

CHAPTER ONE:

YOUR THRONE RIGHTS

When I was a child, Mother had a picture of the princesses Elizabeth and Margaret hanging on a wall of our Australian home. That picture often irritated me. I was envious because they were born royal and I was not. I was annoyed because eventually one of them would be Queen, and thus rule over me. This affronted my budding masculine ego!

Happily those juvenile irritations have long vanished and I am now content to give the Queen the honour due to her as the monarch of my homeland.

But I have also found that God has a marvellous way of making dreams come true. Those early longings for a royal lineage, those aspirations for a kingly throne, have been given an exciting fulfilment - for God has amazingly realised my young fancies. I am proud to announce that he has elevated me to an extraordinary royalty! I say "*extraordinary*", because my rank is not merely that of a modern democratic constitutional monarch, afflicted with much ritual but little power; rather, God has ennobled me with a genuine, ancient, autocratic kingship, heavy with royal prerogatives that are founded on the divine right of its princes!

The throne he has given me is no mere ceremonial piece; it is replete with power, its sceptre is mighty, its dominion as wide as God's own, its crown full of glory. This is a sovereignty like that represented in scripture (the only kind of sovereignty recognised in the ancient world), where the king speaks and the whole earth hastens to do his bidding!

But all who claim royal lineage must be able to produce a patent of their high birth; that is, documentary evidence to establish their right to the throne. Can I do this? Yes, I can. And so can you. For God has granted you the same elevation as he has to me. This enthronement comes to us through Christ, and we have the strongest possible claim to it: it is ours by right of birth**, by right of adoption**, and by right of conquest.

There are those who are kings because they are born with a crown upon their heads; there are those who are kings because they have been adopted **into a royal family; and there are those who have seized a throne by force**. But in all history, only God's chosen people hold the throne by this triple right! Their claim could hardly be more secure. No coup against them can hope to succeed. No insurrection can disturb their dominion. Their sovereignty is invincible!

Your right to the throne is established

- **by the new birth**, which has made you the Father's child.
- **by adoption in Christ**, which has doubly strengthened your legal claim.
- **by conquest**, through your access by faith to the triumph of Christ's resurrection and ascension.

And all of this is confirmed by a set of immutable parchments, your personal "*letters patent*" - the holy scriptures. One passage in particular is outstanding -

> *"Our God is rich in mercy; so out of the great love he had for us, even when we were `dead' because of our sins, he made us alive together with Christ (you are saved by grace). But then, through our union with Christ, God has also raised us up with him and enthroned us with him in `the heavenly places'. His purpose in showing this kindness toward us in Christ Jesus, is that in the coming ages he might reveal the immeasurable riches of his grace" (Ep. 2:4-9, free translation).*

The key statement is the one underlined. It declares that God has "*enthroned us with Christ in the heavenly places*". And this great act was accomplished without any reference to your personal merit. In fact, you had none. At the time of your enthronement you were "*dead*" in your sins. Your glorious elevation comes to you solely by the grace of God. It is his free gift to you in Christ. It results only from the union with Christ God has wrought in you by faith (and you cannot even boast about your faith, for it too is a gift of God!)

So you can neither increase nor destroy your royal prerogatives in Christ; the whole work was completed before you were even born. It is now secure in "*the heavenlies*", beyond harm by devil or man, guaranteed for ever by the resurrection, ascension, and enthronement of Christ.

If you have become united with Christ through faith, then it is true to say that when Christ rose from the dead, you rose with him; when Christ ascended into heaven, you ascended with him; when Christ sat down at the right hand of the majesty on high, you sat down with him; and now with Christ you are enthroned

> *"far above all rule and authority and power and dominion, and above every name that is named, not only in this age, but also in that which is to come!" (Ep 1:20-21).*

Now we see here two things -

GREAT CHANGE

If it is true that you are identified with Christ in his death, burial, resurrection, ascension, and enthronement, then a startling change in life-style is called for. No commoner who has been suddenly elevated to royalty, and who knows this has happened to him, can ever be the same again.

Suppose you discovered today that you were next in succession to the throne of Great Britain, that you would eventually be crowned at Westminster Abbey, and that your residence would then be Buckingham Palace. How your life would change! Knowing that you were the rightful heir to all of the titles, prerogatives, and wealth of the British monarchy, how could you ever again feel poor or insignificant?

Yet that inheritance would be penurious in comparison with the kingly rights God has already given you in Christ! That is subject to the ravages of time; but this will be splendid for eternity. That offers material advantage; but this encompasses not only earthly benefits, but also spiritual treasures, which are infinitely more valuable. That conveys a limited territory, a restricted dominion; but this embraces the authority of God himself.

There is no throne greater than this, no sovereign except God who occupies a higher place. Those whose right it is to sit upon this throne (and all who have come into union with Christ have this right) have received a rule and an authority, a power and a dominion, a name and an honour, which are above any other in time or eternity.

WHAT WE WERE AND WHAT WE ARE

The greatness of this change is almost beyond comprehension! For were we not, like the rest of mankind, "*dead through trespasses and sins*"? Did we not "*follow the course of this world*", yielding allegiance to "*the prince of the power of the air, the spirit that is now at work in the sons of disobedience*"? Were we not among those who live "*in the passions of the flesh, following the desires of body and mind, and so we were by nature children of wrath*"?

But even when we were thus dead to him, God loved us with such a great love, and his mercy was so rich, that he touched us by his grace and made us alive together with Christ (Ep 2:1-5).

An emphasis should be placed on Paul's use of the word "*even*" (vs.5). "*Even when we were dead*" God reached down and raised us up with Christ, and enthroned us with him in the heavenlies. Our case could hardly have been worse. Who is more helpless than a dead man? Who could have been less fit to sit upon a throne, who less deserving of such breathtaking splendour? But God has thus shown the immeasurable riches of his grace toward us in Christ: even when our case was so desperate, and we were so utterly undeserving, he exalted us to the highest conceivable sovereignty!

Now since it is all of God's kindness, works must be excluded. He has not made you a king because of your good deeds; neither will he deny your title because you fail in righteousness.

You cannot fall into a worse state today than you were in when God first made you alive together with Christ. You were "*dead*" then; you cannot be any more "*dead*" now! There are no degrees of death. He who is dead is dead absolutely and irrevocably - except for a miracle of divine grace. This miracle has already been wrought for you in Christ. Your enthronement with Christ could not be destroyed by your sins yesterday, neither will it be destroyed by your sins tomorrow. The work has been fully accomplished through the effort of Christ, not through any effort of yours.

Paul is emphatic: you were dead in sins; you are alive in Christ. The apostle delights in drawing this comparison between what we were and what we are. For example -

> *"For we ourselves were once foolish, disobedient, led astray, slaves to various passions and pleasures, passing our days in malice and envy, hated by men and hating one another; but when the goodness and loving kindness of God our Saviour appeared, he saved us, not because of deeds done by us in righteousness, but in virtue of his own mercy ... so that we might be justified by his grace and become heirs in hope of eternal life. This saying is sure" (Tit 3:3-8).*

Note again that your salvation and inheritance do not depend in any way upon anything you can do. It is not by virtue of your good works, but by virtue of his grace that you have been accorded such a magnificent status. Paul is so keen for his readers to grasp this, he emphasises it: "*This saying is true!*" You must believe it. No matter how dead you may have been in sin, in Christ God has made you alive! Your part is to accept this new identity, and to begin to live it out.

A NEW EVALUATION

It is important to realise that Paul is describing our condition as God sees it. When he talks about "*what we were*" and "*what we are*" he is talking from a divine perspective. He is saying that God once saw us in sin, foolish, disobedient, slaves to passion (and so on), even if we did not see ourselves that way; but now God sees us in Christ, alive, enthroned, victorious (and so on), even if we do not see ourselves this way. We have to learn to accept God's judgment of our situation, and not our own.

Irrespective of some good things you may have done, God saw you then as dead in trespasses and sins; but now, irrespective of some bad things you may do, God sees you as alive in Christ. You may then have had seeming success in avoiding certain sins; but God nonetheless saw in you only desperate defeat. You may now seem to be defeated by certain sins; but God sees in you only glorious victory. You may then have thought yourself a king, but in God's reckoning you were a slave; you may now think yourself a slave, but in God's reckoning you are a king.

Our problem is this: our assessment of a situation is rarely the same as God's!

And nowhere is that more so than when we face the divine declaration that we have been raised with Christ and enthroned with him in the heavenlies.

You have to stop looking at yourself with a natural eye and see yourself as God sees you. Your personal evaluation of yourself is not worth anything. The only assessment that is worth anything is God's. He will deal with you on the basis of what he thinks about you, not on the basis of what you think. And God has resolved never to see you independently of Christ. He sees you only as you are mirrored in Christ. As Christ is, so God sees you, and so he reckons you to be.

If you want to get anywhere with God you will have to start thinking the way he thinks and saying what he says; and he says that although you were once dead in your iniquity, now through your union with Christ you are already raised into the heavenlies and seated with Christ on his glorious throne!

But no king will act like a king, nor enjoy the privileges of his royal rank, if he refuses to accept his identity.

Go back for a moment to my illustration about the British monarchy. Suppose you have been notified that documents recently discovered prove beyond all doubt that you are the rightful heir to the throne of England. But suppose also that you refuse to believe the herald. You greet his announcement with scorn. You give a thousand reasons for your disbelief - your obviously humble birth, your lack of the manners of royalty, your incapacity to rule, your reluctance to abandon your present life, and so on. No one can force you to take up the sceptre. So your crown by default will go to another.

Likewise, God will not compel you to accept your enthronement with Christ. If you persistently refuse to take up the rod of authority, if you are determined to keep up the pretence of being a commoner (to maintain your belief that you are still "*dead*" in sins), if you shun the new position God has given you in Christ, then you simply nullify the grace of God. You will certainly remain impoverished and defeated.

Then there are those who do assume their rights, and they sit down on the throne; but in due course some circumstance arises that drives them to abdicate - as Edward VIII abandoned the English throne in 1936 to marry Bessie Simpson, his American sweetheart. So these Christians begin well, affirming with zest their rights and authority in Christ, but pressure comes, or their circumstances change, and suddenly they abdicate, convinced they are no longer fit to be kings.

But we have to understand the triple right to the throne that I mentioned above, and that God has freely granted us in Christ. That right cannot now be lawfully taken away from us. We can lose it only by personal default or abdication - that is, either by refusing to accept our new position in Christ, or by abandoning the throne after we have assumed the crown.

Thus hardly anything is more important than that you should refuse to look at yourself from a natural and earthly perspective. The testimony of scripture concerning the new identity and privileges God has given you in Christ must be heartily accepted. Change the way you think about yourself! Refuse to accept any judgment of your situation except God's! The world may say you are weak and insignificant; the devil may denounce you as fraudulent and hypocritical; you may condemn yourself as sinful and unclean. But none of those opinions have any weight with God. Learn to evaluate yourself, not according to your human condition, but according to divine revelation. Ultimately, reality is found only in what God says. Any other assessment is false.

No wonder Paul writes: "*Do not be conformed to this world, but be transformed by the renewing of your mind*" (Ro 12:2). Transformation of your life, from defeat to victory, from sickness to health, from poverty to riches, from sin to righteousness, from death to life, begins with a renewed mind. Think God's thoughts! Then what is "*good and acceptable and perfect*" will be wrought in you. Heed the scripture that says "*take every thought captive to obey Christ*" (2 Co 10:4-5). Think well of yourself in Christ, for, in Christ, God thinks well of you.

You are a king. Think like one.

A GREAT CONFESSION

What you most truly believe you will inevitably say. "*Out of the abundance of the heart the mouth speaks*" (Mt 12:34). But it is also true that "*the abundance of the heart*" can be shaped by what the mouth says. What you believe you will speak, but what you speak will change what you believe.

So in this matter of your throne rights there must be an interplay of believing and speaking. Thinking like a king and speaking like a king must go hand in hand. If you believe it you will speak it; if you speak it you will believe it. Heart belief and spoken confession arise from each other and establish and strengthen each other.

In Christian life faith can never go beyond confession, while a right confession enhances faith and takes it further than it would otherwise have gone.

Since then you now believe that you are a king, you must also talk like one. So speak with authority against your spiritual enemy and against everything belonging to the kingdom of darkness.

This faith-confession is the army and weaponry of our kingdom. The spoken word is our best method of attack and of defence.

The Roman centurion said to Jesus, "Speak the word only, and my servant will be healed." But now the situation is reversed. Now Christ says to you, "Stand your ground in faith; you speak the word only, in my name, and victory will be yours!" Your miracle is in your mouth. Speak it and it will happen!

When you think as God thinks, and say what God says, then you attract to yourself the infinite resources of heaven, you release the wealth and power of your heavenly throne, and the forces of Satan tremble.

The throne upon which God has placed you in Christ will wax powerful and mighty, or it will be rendered weak and ineffectual (for you), depending on the degree of boldness of your faith-confession. Speak up, like a king! Speak with authority, like a great monarch! Assert your throne rights, boldly and persistently. Yield to no opposition. Accept no defeat. Identify yourself in Christ. Take your seat upon the throne. Lay claim to all of the marvellous privileges, and to the spiritual dominion, that God has freely given you in his Son.

But now two questions arise: what is the nature of this faith-confession; and how is it affected by sin?

The nature of our faith-*confession*, what its content should be, where it is appropriate, or inappropriate, to speak with authority, will become apparent in the chapters that follow. At this point, I want to answer only the second question: "*Will sin not dethrone me?*"

If you wilfully and deliberately continue to indulge in some sin, without shame or any real desire to be rid of it, then you may well be destroyed, cut off without hope, turned back into darkness and death.[1] Any sin, when pressed to an extreme of rebellion against God, and of hardness of heart, will cut the sinner off from Christ. He is no longer "*in Christ*". He is isolated from salvation. He becomes as though he had never repented, nor ever believed. He is a heathen again, and no longer a Christian. He has plainly forfeited all of his throne rights.

But it is not easy for a person who has once truly believed in the Lord Jesus Christ, who has truly been "*turned from darkness to light, and from the power of Satan to God*", who has been born again, to fall utterly back into spiritual death. The grace of God is difficult to resist. The Holy Spirit strives to rescue the endangered soul. It takes more than one sin, or even a hundred, to slay God's children, to put them outside of Christ, and to invalidate their throne rights.

Remember, God does not call you his child because you have done well, but because Christ did well. His merits, not yours, are the

---

[1] See, for example, the solemn warnings in He 3:12-14; 4:11; 6:4-8; 10:26-31; 12:15-17.

basis of your enthronement. So long as you cling to him, despite the sin that may overtake you from time to time, then your spiritual authority, and your rights and privileges, will all remain undisturbed.

If you sin, then, you do not honour God, nor please him, by lying in a fallen state, wallowing in misery, bewailing your weakness.

Your proper part is to repent the moment you are challenged to do so by the Holy Spirit, to trust at once in the pardoning grace of God, and to affirm more vigorously than before your complete victory in Christ.

Indeed, the more boldly you declare your kingly status, the more difficult it will be for sin to topple you again. So your faith-confession should not be controlled by your experience; rather you should say what God says about you, in Christ, regardless of your experience. The more you say it, the more you will live it.

God has not enthroned you in the heavenlies because of your achievements in overcoming sin, but because of what Christ has done. Your righteousness did not put you on the throne, your unrighteousness (unless it is pressed to the extreme point of severing you from Christ) cannot thrust you off the throne. In Christ (not in yourself) you are rescued from death, raised up into heaven, and seated on the throne. God demands that you believe this because he has said it, whether or not it is happening in your daily life. And having believed it, God then demands that you boldly confess it - in the face of sin, into the teeth of Satan, despite weakness, over the head of defeat. He requires you to say aloud what he says you are in Christ. Your word of faith will bring into reality in your daily life what is already true of you in the heavenlies.

CHAPTER TWO:

IN THE HEAVENLIES

There is an ineluctable spiritual law which says that faith must precede practice. Many Christians fail to live victoriously because they try to reverse that law to read: practice first, then faith. But spiritual law is as unremitting as natural law. The rule cannot be violated: faith must come before practice. That is, before you can **behave** like a saint you must **believe** that you are a saint!

Christ stated this law in his saying, "*You will know the truth and the truth will make you free*" (Jn 8:32).

Here is something we all want: freedom to serve God, to love him, to rejoice in his goodness; freedom in worship and prayer; freedom to live righteously, to walk soberly and godly in this present world; freedom from sickness, and from every dark work; freedom to prosper every day in the favour of God.

How can we obtain that freedom?

Jesus said simply, "*Know the truth!*"

In other words, before you begin to pray for some need to be met, first get hold of what God says about his willingness and ability to meet that need, and then believe God's word with all your heart. Your knowledge of, and faith in, the word of God, is the initial key to all of his wonderful treasures.

This law is applied continually in the NT. Before explaining Christian practice the apostles almost invariably explained Christian belief ....

In Romans, Paul wrote eleven chapters of powerful argument on the plan of salvation before adding five chapters on practical living.

In Galatians, the closing two chapters of warning, instruction, and exhortation, are preceded by four chapters of closely reasoned faith, climaxed by the pungent challenge, "*Stand fast in the freedom by which Christ has made us free!*" Not until he had brought the Galatians onto the ground of full Christian liberty did Paul tell them how to display the characteristics of a true Christian. Faith before practice!

In Ephesians, Paul begins with three breathtaking chapters that show the glories of Christ, the immensity of salvation, and the vast scope of God's plan for the church. He explores the infinite wealth of the gospel, and reveals the riches of grace and glory God has given us in Christ. Then, and not before, does he begin a practical application of the truth. He was careful to declare what God has done for us before writing what we have to do for God.

In many other places in the NT the same principle can be observed. Before urging Christian duties the apostles were always careful to teach the people Christian doctrine.

This rule is particularly obvious in Paul's written prayers. An apostle praying for the church - what will be the theme of his intercession? Will he pray that they might conquer sin? or be healed? or that the church will grow? or that their needs might be met?

No! He prayed for none of the things that fill the prayers of most Christians. He pleaded with passion, not that they might be given things, but that they might know the truth. Again and again, he longed for them to know ... know ... **KNOW**!

With fervent intercession he prayed that God would give them wisdom and revelation in the knowledge of Christ; that they might know the hope of their calling and the riches of God's glory; that they might understand the limitless power available to them in Christ; that they might comprehend the love of God, and perceive his will, and gain spiritual illumination - see Ep 1:15- 19; 3:14-19; Ph 1:9-10; Col 1:9; etc.

Paul knew, if people familiarise themselves with the truth in Christ, if they steep themselves in knowledge of the gospel, if they grasp the significance of all that Christ wrought at Calvary for their full salvation, then they need nothing else. All the things they might desire will come to them as a natural consequence of this knowledge of the truth.

Perhaps the most thrilling presentation of the wealth God has freely given us in Christ is found in the first three chapters of Paul's letter to the Ephesians. In this letter Paul fathoms the utmost depths, and scales the transcendent heights, of the glories of the gospel, and he reveals them to us in five pungent sayings about our position IN THE HEAVENLIES in Christ - Ep 1:3,20; 2:6; 3:10; 6:12.

YOUR PROVISION IN THE HEAVENLIES

> *"Blessed be the God and Father of our Lord Jesus Christ, who has blessed us in Christ with every spiritual blessing <u>in the heavenlies</u>" (Ep 1:3).*

For a Christian, "*to believe*" means to accept without reservation the witness God has given of himself in scripture. In particular, I am challenged to accept two things: what the Bible says about Christ; and what the Bible says about me. To believe the first without the second is to have a truncated faith, one that will deny me access to the best part of God's blessings.

If I am content to accept the witness of scripture about the identity of Christ in God, then I should also be willing to accept what it says about my identity in Christ. The one has little value without the other.

Nowhere is this principle more apparent than in Paul's use of the phrase "*in the heavenlies*".

No one is really sure what that phrase means, except that it evidently describes a particular spiritual dimension into which we have gained access by Christ. In this place, God has deposited all the treasures of salvation; here, every spiritual blessing is located in abundance. Whatever you need from God, whatever God wants to give, is placed here already in your name.

EVERY BLESSING IS ALREADY YOURS

You will notice, Paul says this great work has already been done. This is not a promise. It is a statement of fact: "*God has blessed us with every spiritual blessing in the heavenlies.*"

You say you have need of blessing? But God has already blessed you!

And what has he given you? It is nothing less than "*every spiritual blessing*"!

Can you even begin to enumerate the profuse supply indicated by that statement? Can you ever exhaust that limitless treasure? All spiritual blessings! All the good things you have ever longed for and prayed for! Every blessing the human heart could desire, and every kindness divine hands can provide. All the riches of glory, and all the stores of earth. For your body, all health, ability, and victory. For your mind, all understanding, satisfaction, and belief. For your soul, all cleansing, salvation, and life. For your spirit, all illumination, faith, and quickening!

With such superlative provision the Lord God has already blessed you.

But, you say, "I do not see that I have all these things!"

Perhaps you have looked in the wrong place? Where are all these spiritual blessings to be found? In yourself? In your church? In your own good works? The scripture tells us quite plainly where to locate them: God has blessed us with every spiritual blessing "*in the heavenlies.*"

Here then is a particular realm, known as "*the heavenlies*" where you have unlimited credit. In this place, deposited in your name, is untold wealth. It is yours now! If you and I are not enjoying this divine provision it is only because we are not looking in the right place or approaching by the right way.

Suppose there was a commercial bank called "*The Bank of the Heavenlies*". If a friend deposited a large sum of money in that bank, in your name, you would at once become wealthy. But your new wealth would do you no good unless you went to that particular bank, presented an authority that gave you the right to draw on the money, and then withdrew from the account as much as you required.

So it is with your riches in God's "*heavenlies*" - you must enter this spiritual dimension with the right authority and claim what is yours by faith. How to do this will be explained as this chapter continues; but first let us look more closely at ....

THE MEANING OF "SPIRITUAL BLESSINGS"

What are these "*spiritual blessings*" Paul is talking about?

It would be wrong to think of them as blessings that are "*spiritual*" in contrast with physical and material blessings. They are called "*spiritual*" blessings, not because they are unearthly, but because they have a spiritual basis - that is, they arise from the ministry of the Holy Spirit in the Christian's life; they stem from our union with Christ.[2]

But the blessings themselves comprehend every promise God has ever given us of pardon, healing, victory, supply, and so on.

Paul gives a kind of analysis of these blessings in Ep 1:3-20. He lists them as

- a blameless and holy life (vs. 4)
- destiny as the sons of God (vs. 5-6)

---

[2] At least 10 times in the first chapter of Ephesians, Paul uses the expression "*in Christ*" or "*through Christ*" = union with Christ by faith.

- redemption and forgiveness (vs. 7-8)
- knowledge of the plan of God (vs. 9-10)[3]
- freedom to live for God's glory (vs. 11-12)
- the promise of the Holy Spirit (vs. 13)
- a guaranteed inheritance (vs. 14)

Then he sums it all up in three great statements (vs. 18-20)

- the hope to which he has called us
- the riches of his glorious inheritance
- the immeasurable greatness of his power

Hope, riches, great power: those three words embrace every spiritual blessing God has provided for you in the heavenlies

1. there is hope: for our future is secure in Christ. We have a destiny, a kingdom, a reward appointed for us, of which none can deprive us, save we ourselves, by unbelief.
2. there are riches: of pardon, of grace, of healing, of life, of supply of every need; indeed, all the treasures offered in the good promises of God.
3. there is power, immeasurably great power: over all of the kingdom of darkness, over the principalities and powers of evil, over sin, over the opposition of the world, over death and the very gates of hell.

Two keys are needed to unlock these treasures -

[3] If this was the only benefit of the gospel (apart from forgiveness of sin) I would still be filled with joy. To me, this is one of the chief blessings of God: the revelation he has given us of his great purpose, the assurance that life is not a mindless jumble of random events, but that it has a divinely appointed goal, toward which the entire creation is inexorably moving.

1 - REVELATION

As I have already indicated, our ears and eyes need to be opened so that we might understand that all of these promised blessings are ours right now. These are not future promises; they are present possessions!

But such knowledge is beyond the natural mind. It must be revealed by the Spirit. A merely mental understanding of the promise is not enough; these things must be spiritually perceived.

People can read, say, the first chapter of Ephesians, and mentally agree with every word, yet remain as impoverished before God as ever they were. It has to get from the mind into the heart. "*With the heart a man believes*" and so obtains the blessing of God (Ro 10:8-10).

If it was enough merely to read the promise, and to accept it in your mind as true, then Paul, having just instructed the Ephesians (1:13-14), would not have said immediately, "*Now I am going to pray that God will reveal these things to you!*"

He knew that his written words, no matter how sincerely they might be received, were insufficient by themselves. The touch of God was needed to make those words come alive in the hearts of the people. The people needed an inner revelation of the truth of what was written. So, having described all of these spiritual blessings which belong to the people of God in the heavenlies, Paul at once began to pray -

> *"May the God of our Lord Jesus Christ, the Father of glory, give you a spirit of wisdom and of revelation in the knowledge of him, having the eyes of your heart enlightened, that you may know .... " (vs. 15-18).*

That is divinely imparted knowledge. It is head knowledge become heart knowledge. It is knowledge perceived by a spiritual quickening of the things the mind has received. What has been "*heard*" by the ear is now "*seen*" in the spirit. It is the Lord opening the eyes of your heart, giving you spiritual illumination, so that his word suddenly becomes to you the only reality.

All other knowledge is overwhelmed by this inner knowledge of the promise of God. By divine revelation you grasp his presence and power, and your faith laughs at every foe, and rejoices in the sure victory of God (cp. 2 Kg 6:15-17).

This spiritual insight comes to people in different ways - sometimes while reading scripture; sometimes while sitting under the preaching of the word; or in some other way.

But pre-eminently it comes by taking up a promise of God and praying over that promise until the Lord does impart "*a spirit of wisdom and of revelation in the knowledge of him*".

But whatever way it comes, there is simply no substitute for "*having the eyes of your heart enlightened*". Without this, the promises of God will remain for you a dead letter.

How will you know when it has happened? You will know, because you will know! That is, the promise of God will not be merely something you have memorised; it will now be as real as life itself. You will have an awareness, deep within, that the promise of God is irresistibly true. Incredulity will change to total belief. The hiatus between you and the promise will be bridged. The credibility gap will no longer exist. You and the promise will be fused together. It will be inconceivable to you that the promise could fail.

This change is something like what you might experience if you were told by a stranger that he was about to give you a million dollars. At first you would be incredulous, perhaps even angry at his seeming attempt to mock you. But he insists that you take his check, and he is so earnest and sincere you begin to have second thoughts. You finally take the check and, hardly daring to hope, go off to the bank against which it is drawn. You enquire at the bank, and to your utter astonishment discover that the check is good, and the money is yours whenever you want it. Now all doubt is gone!

Now you know! Suddenly the truth of it strikes you! What merriment fills your heart! At once you begin to think and talk differently, for now you know that you are truly a millionaire!

That same kind of assurance has to come to you concerning the riches God has laid up for you in the heavenlies, and it will bring the same kind of gladness. Those riches are yours now, if you can believe it.

2 - RELEASE

If "*revelation*" is the first key to unlock your spiritual blessings in the heavenlies, then the second key is the "*release*" of your faith. Those things that are already your potential possessions will become your actual possessions when you make a faith commitment to receive them from God.

This faith must be specific. You cannot reasonably expect to reach out and grasp every spiritual blessing in one moment any more than you can eat a whole warehouse full of food in one meal. You need to determine which is the proper spiritual blessing for you at the present time, and then to release your faith in God for that one thing.

People frequently fail to obtain the spiritual blessing they need, because they are too vague in their application of the promise. Real faith cannot function until a particular promise is applied to a particular need.

For example, people say, "*I know that God can meet my financial needs.*" But that is more a statement of doctrinal belief than of specific faith. Real faith would say, "*I know God will send me the money to pay this bill!*" In fact, real faith would be even more bold: "*I know God has already blessed me with the money for this bill in the heavenlies in Christ!*"

- Faith possesses its possessions!
- Faith rejoices in the provision God has already made!

- Faith shouts with gladness, "Blessed be the God and Father of our Lord Jesus Christ, who has blessed us in Christ with every spiritual blessing in the heavenlies."

YOUR POWER IN THE HEAVENLIES

> *"God raised Christ from the dead and made him sit at his right hand in the heavenlies" (1:20).*

Take particular note of the magnificent prayer Paul offered in connection with this statement about Christ's ascension into the heavenlies:

> *"I pray that you might know the immeasurable greatness of his power in us who believe, according to the working of his great might which he accomplished in Christ when he raised him from the dead" (vs.19).*

He did not ask God to give them power. He longed only that they might know the greatness of God's power in the heavenlies, and know that this power, all of it, was already their possession and prerogative.

What is this power? How does it become ours?

THE MEASURE OF THIS POWER

Paul measures this power which is ours in the heavenlies, and tells us two things about its greatness

firstly: it is "*immeasurable*"; no Christian need ever fear that this power will be insufficient to meet any difficulty that may arise.

secondly: it is "*according to*" a particular demonstration of the might of God. What was this? The power available to each Christian is "*according to the working of the mighty power which God wrought in Christ when he raised him from the dead*".

So the extraordinary strength that we own in the heavenlies is the same in character, force, and effect as that which broke the bonds of death from the crucified Christ, freed him from sin's darkness, and raised him in glory to heaven's radiant throne!

It is interesting to compare the standards of power of the old dispensation and the new.

Before the resurrection of Christ, whenever men wanted to depict the power of God, they could cite no greater demonstration than the exodus of Israel from Egypt. Again and again the prophets used that striking event as the supreme example of God's power. The exodus showed what tremendous things the Lord could do for those who trusted him. The measure of divine ability in the old dispensation was "*according to*" Israel's deliverance from Egyptian tyranny.

But now there is a new standard. Now we are given an infinitely higher measure of revealed omnipotence. It is found in the resurrection and ascension of Christ. The manifestation of God's power in the former time was great, but now it is immeasurably great! It took the working of his power to bring Israel out of Egypt, but it was the working of his mighty power that raised Christ from the dead and set him at the right hand of the majesty on high!

There is also a contrast between the effectiveness of the old power and the new. If the first was a physical deliverance from temporal bondage, the second is spiritual freedom from eternal death. If the first wrought national liberty, the second has created salvation for the entire race. If the first offered Israel an earthly inheritance and natural wealth, the second has opened to all who believe the unlimited storehouse of God, and a kingdom eternal in the heavens!

THE PURPOSE AND LOCATION OF THIS POWER

The power of God is at once nullified if any attempt is made to use it in situations other than those approved by God. It is limitless power, irresistible in heaven and on earth; but it is not available to any person for any purpose. It is not like an unshielded electric power socket, open for anyone to plug into whenever they please!

The power of God cannot be used to do the will of man; it is available only to accomplish the will of God. No one can appropriate this power to do merely his own pleasure; but the believer can and should appropriate it to do all that he knows is the pleasure of God.

Hence Paul writes -

> *"May you be strengthened with all power, according to his glorious might ... to lead a life worthy of the Lord, fully pleasing to him, bearing fruit in every good work ... for all endurance and patience with joy" (Col 1:9-11).*

So this glorious might of God - the same might that raised Christ from the dead - is available right now to strengthen you to accomplish all that lies in God's purpose for your life. You need never feel inadequate for any situation into which you are brought by obedience to God. In the strength of his power within you (that power which you draw from "*the heavenlies*"), you can do whatever God has appointed - whether to

> *"conquer kingdoms, enforce justice, receive promises, stop the mouths of lions, quench raging fire, escape the edge of the sword, win strength out of weakness, become mighty in war, put armies to flight, raise the dead"; or to "endure torture, refusing to accept release, suffer mocking, scourging, chains, imprisonment, destitution, affliction, ill-treatment, death" (cp. He 11:32-38).*

Once I have discovered the will of God in any situation then his power is mine to do his will - whether to change that situation by a miracle, or to endure it with steadfast patience!

Since the power of God exists only to do the will of God, this power is not carelessly left where anyone may improperly abuse it. It has been drawn up with Christ (when God raised him from the dead), and it remains with him, secure in the heavenlies. It is not there, however, for his benefit, but for ours. It is not extended toward the angels; it belongs to "*us who believe*", and towards us it is proffered.

Moses had his rod. It was offered to him by God, and he took it up. It became for him the guarantee of God's power. By that rod, and by the signs and wonders it produced, he smashed imperial Egypt and created an example that for many centuries was the summit of God's power among men.

Do you envy Moses his privilege? Do you stand in wonder before that staggering display of divine omnipotence? It certainly should be admired; yet that ancient example has been overwhelmingly surpassed by God's stupendous new feat in Christ! And now, right now, offered to you who believe, as surely as the rod was proffered to Moses, is the right to grasp the enormous power that wrenched Christ from death and exalted him to the highest glory!

In the heavenlies, Christ reigns in splendid authority,

> *"far above all rule and authority and power and dominion, and above every name that is named, not only in this age but also in that which is to come" (Ep 1:21).*

What incredible majesty!

But here is the most marvellous thing: this victory was not accomplished for heaven's benefit, but for yours!

God had no need to establish his power over the devil, for that was done in the very beginning, when Satan was thrown out of the garden of Eden.

Nor did Christ personally need to be exalted above the kingdom of darkness; for he had long before cast down Lucifer and the angels who rebelled with him, leaving them bound in chains of darkness.

Christ was raised from the dead, and lifted into the heavenlies, not to establish heaven's power (which was never at risk), but to establish power for us who believe in Christ. This "*immeasurably great*" power is not meant to be a weapon in God's hand, but a mighty resource in your hands, so that you, in the mighty name of Jesus, might be fully delivered from the oppression of Satan.

It is indeed true that "*God has put all things under Christ's feet*" (vs 22). But why? For your benefit, and mine! For he goes on to say: " *... and has made him head of all things for the church.*"

On behalf of the church, God raised Jesus from the dead. On behalf of the church, Christ was exalted on high. On behalf of the church, he now reigns in the heavenlies. On behalf of the church, everything has been placed under his feet.

But if you are part of his church, then you also are there, in the heavenlies, with Christ. All the power that is his, is yours. Here then is victory over the prince of evil, deliverance from the grip of sin, liberty from the dominion of temptation, healing from the imprisonment of disease. It is all found by seizing what is already yours in the heavenlies.

Paul waxes even more bold. So sure is he of our complete identification with Christ, so certain we are already seated with Christ in the heavenlies, he declares that this immeasurably great power is even now "*in us who believe.*" Yes, it is IN you at this moment. You may not feel it, but you can believe it! And if you believe it, then that power will begin at once to fulfil God's marvellous work in your life.

Do you find it hard to believe that the resurrection power of Jesus is in you right now? Paul gives an illustration that clinches the matter. He says,

> *"God has put all things under Christ's feet and has made him head over all things for the church, which is his body, the fullness of him who fills all in all" (vs. 22,23).*

If Christ is the Head, and we are his body, then where he is we must be also; what he is we must be also; what he has must be ours also. How can it be otherwise? Christ is no monstrosity. He is not deformed.

Consider your own body: where your head is, your body is. In natural life, every good thing your body is to receive enters the body by the head - through the mouth, the eyes, the ears - and then is shared by the whole body.

So also, all the fullness of Christ, the Head, belongs to the church, his body: "*The church is the fullness of him who fills all in all.*" What is given to the Head, Christ, inevitably belongs also to his body, the church, and hence to every "*member*" of that body.

So then, if you have come into union with Christ through faith, all of his heavenly power is now yours as much as it is his. Only unbelief can block its mighty flow. But if you can believe it, then his resurrection power is in your hands when you lay them on the sick in his name; it is in your voice when you speak that word of faith and authority; it is in your mind as you search out the wisdom of God in scripture; it is in your flesh as you stand against the kingdom of darkness and seize the triumph of God. It permeates your entire being; it is the law of life in Christ Jesus setting you free from the law of sin and death!

Those sentences lead irresistibly to the next text -

YOUR POSITION IN THE HEAVENLIES

> *"God has made us alive together with Christ, and through our union with Christ by faith, he has raised us up and enthroned us with Christ in the heavenlies" (2:5-6, free translation).*

There is a difference between what might be called "*situational*" truth and "*positional*" truth.

Situational truth describes your condition at the present time, that is, your situation as observed by the natural eye. It is the state you are apparently in just now, whether spiritual, mental, emotional, or physical. It is the way you feel, the condition of your health, the measure of your finances, the extent of victory or defeat you may be experiencing. It tells the facts about your present circumstances, what is actually happening in your life day by day.

Positional truth describes your condition as God sees it in Christ. It is your position in the heavenlies in contrast with your situation on earth. On earth, you may be incomplete in sin; but in the heavenlies you are complete in Christ (Col 2:10).

The Bible in fact declares four things about your "*position*"

1. you are <u>crucified</u> with Christ

   that is, united with him in his atoning death, thus becoming the recipient of all the mercy, pardon, and grace made available to each repentant sinner at Calvary.

2. you are <u>risen</u> with Christ

   that is, united with him in his victory over the power of sin, the strength of death, and the grip of the grave.

3. you are <u>ascended</u> with Christ

   that is, united with him in his endless life and in his unlimited access to the throne of God.

4. you are <u>enthroned</u> with Christ

   that is, united with him in his triumph over Satan, and over all the powers of darkness, and over all that is antagonistic to the kingdom of God.

Now you must realise that those events are not set in the future; rather, they are true of you NOW! They describe the position you already hold in Christ. This is how God sees you at this moment! Not in isolation, of course, but as you are in Christ.

In the reckoning of God, whatever Christ accomplished through his crucifixion, resurrection, ascension, and enthronement, belongs to you already. When Christ died, God saw you dying. When Christ rose from the dead, God saw you rising. When Christ ascended into heaven, God saw you ascending. When Christ sat down upon his glorious throne, God saw you sitting there.

In the matter of your salvation, all that Christ is, God reckons you to be.

Naturally, if God looked at you apart from Christ, he would not see you crucified, risen, enthroned; on the contrary, he might see you defeated by sin, sick, and oppressed. But he has resolved never to look at any believer apart from Christ. Every time he sees you, he sees you in the virtue of Christ. You are identified in the mind of God with Christ's perfections and triumph.

Now we are told these things, not to establish a pretty theory nor a cosy doctrine, but to provide a basis upon which we can embrace the ability of God in our daily lives. God's desire is obviously that what is true of you and me positionally may become true practically. We are told what we have become in the heavenlies only so that we might become the same on earth.

Here then is a great decision taken in the councils of heaven: God has resolved to position in the heavenlies and upon the throne every person who believes in Christ. This is a spiritual enthronement, wrought in conjunction with the ascension and glorification of Christ, and established irrevocably by God's own infallible declaration in scripture. He has also declared that knowledge of this "*position*" is the legal and practical basis on which the believer will gain victory and fullness in his daily life.

It is the <u>legal</u> basis, because our union with Christ in the heavenlies, through faith, frees us from the reach of God's broken law, and enables him righteously to answer our prayers and to act on our behalf as Saviour (instead of acting against us as Judge).

It is the practical basis, because God has promised to respond in power to every person who grasps the truth of the heavenly position he has given to the believer, and who affirms that position with bold faith.

When you know, regardless of your actual situation on earth, that you truly are spiritually enthroned in the heavenlies with Christ, and when you begin to confess aloud that enthronement, then God will begin to make it actually happen for you.

Here is a law: ***when your confession matches your position, then your situation will be made to match your position. Change your confession, and your situation will also change***.

But many people want to reverse that rule: their attitude is that they will not profess to be enthroned with Christ in the heavenlies until they actually see themselves living like a king on earth. But in God's economy profession always precedes possession.

So, if you say that you are defeated and enslaved, you will effectively disannul your enthronement. But if you say that you are enthroned and triumphant in Christ, then you will effectively disannul your enslavement!

What God declares you to be now, in Christ, you should now reckon yourself to be. If you reckon yourself to be seated on your throne in the heavenlies, then you will also be able to profess yourself to be a king, and to begin to act like one on earth. You cannot stay experimentally on the throne if your reckoning and profession are wrong.

You must think about yourself as God thinks about you. You must get a mental image of yourself that reflects what you are in the heavenlies, not what you are on earth. No matter what your earthly state might be, you must declare yourself by faith to be now all that God says you are in Christ.

WARFARE IN THE HEAVENLIES

"We are not contending against flesh and blood, but against Principalities and Powers" (6:12).

Someone will protest that to say you are enthroned when in fact you are enslaved is to tell a lie. But that is not so. You are merely supplanting one set of facts for another set of greater facts; you are changing one truth by the application of another truth.

An example: for centuries mankind was bound by the obvious fact that iron and steel cannot float, they have no natural buoyancy. So everybody scoffed at the idea of an iron ship. But then somebody was bold enough to apply the laws of displacement and of specific gravity, and, behold! the world was amazed to see an iron ship afloat! The fact that iron sinks in water was overcome by a greater fact: if the weight of the iron vessel is less than that of the water it displaces, it will float.

Likewise, nobody can deny the truth of your situation, which may be one of sin, fear, sickness, or defeat. But then, I am not suggesting that you should deny it. What you should do is replace situational truth with positional truth. Whichever one you choose to believe has power to nullify the other.

The choice is entirely yours.

If you decide to cling to your situation, to talk only about your poverty and failure, to believe that your situation represents the dominant fact in your life, then you will never gain an experimental knowledge of your enthronement in the heavenlies.

But if you decide to accept your rightful position in Christ, and by faith to step up to the throne, confidently affirming and insisting upon your throne rights, then all that God has wrought for you in Christ will become experimentally yours.

Here is another illustration. Let us suppose that a letter has come to you, saying that you have inherited a vast estate in a foreign country. The name of the estate is "*The Heavenlies*". It comprises a million acres of prime grazing and agricultural land, stocked with thousands of quality sheep and cattle. It also contains many beautiful buildings and a vast quantity of machinery; it has huge investments in many industries, and enormous capital reserves. The wealth of the estate is almost incalculable.

Now, assuming you are a person of modest income, that letter represents a truth that has power to utterly transform your present situation. All you have to do is claim what is yours.

But suppose you think the letter is a hoax, or perhaps are fearful of so much wealth and power, so that you refuse to claim what is yours, and in fact you throw the letter away? Or, suppose you allow a false claimant to usurp your title, or an unscrupulous lawyer to contest your claim and to impoverish you?

Many people fail to obtain "*every spiritual blessing*" for just those reasons. They simply cannot believe that this inheritance, this kingly right, is already theirs. Or else they have such an image of personal defeat, they cannot bring themselves to think, speak, and act like an enthroned monarch. Or else they allow the usurper, Satan, by force or guile to deprive them of their inheritance.

So Paul, having said that "*every spiritual blessing*" is found in the heavenlies, also says that we will have to contend for those blessings against the thievery and usurpation of "*principalities spiritual hosts of wickedness.*"

But how should you contend against that deceiver, Satan, and his dark hordes? From the weakness of your earthly situation, or from the strength of your heavenly position? If you are wise, you will possess the throne first, in the name of the invincible Christ, and then war against Satan with a crown on your head and a sceptre in your hand!

Our weapons are not carnal, not "*flesh and blood*", but they are mighty through God to pull down every stronghold of Satan (2 Co 10:3). Even when Paul speaks about us donning our armour and sallying forth to battle, he is careful to show that we fight, not with natural energy or weaponry, but with spiritual resources:

> *"take up the shield of faith and the sword of the Spirit, which is the word of God" (Ep 6:16-17).*

Search and see. Always you will find it is faith and the word!

Go back for a moment to my illustration about inheriting a magnificent estate. Suppose you refused to be intimidated either by the splendour of the inheritance, or by the threats and accusations of a usurper. You are determined to possess your possessions (Ob 17). What would you do? Sit down wringing your hands and decrying your wretched situation? I hope not! Rather you would establish your unquestionable identity as the rightful owner, then you would boldly lay claim to your estate, and march onto it and possess the land, driving off any false claimants who stood in your way. If necessary you would call on the authorities to come to your assistance, and to evict any trespassers.

You should do the same for your heavenly estate.

Get your identity right to begin with. Are you truly a Christian? Are you the actual person Paul was speaking about when he said "*you were made alive together with Christ, and raised up with him, and made to sit with him in the heavenlies*" (Ep 2:5-6)? If you are, then you have an unassailable right to the throne. Press your identity against the enemy. Put up your shield of faith against his accusations. Fall upon him with the word of God. Call for the legions of heaven, those "*ministering spirits*" (He 1:14), to hasten to your assistance. Give your enemy no quarter, nor rest your demands, until he leaves you in undisputed possession of your rightful inheritance.

Those who sit upon a throne have throne rights. God says that by virtue of your union with Christ you are at this moment enthroned in the heavenlies. So exercise your rights, and be oppressed by Satan no more!

TAKING YOUR RIGHTFUL PLACE

Although I have suggested that "*the heavenlies*" describes a special kind of spiritual location, I do not want to infer that you have to go looking for this place. You do not have to go anywhere to be in "*the heavenlies*", you only need to be in Christ.

Neither do you have to be anything, or become anything, different from what you are just now. The immense privileges and power God has provided in the heavenlies are reserved for none except the sinner who believes in Christ.

Paul identifies those who are the proper beneficiaries of the heavenly inheritance, and he describes them as those who are "*dead through trespasses and sins*", who are "*sons of disobedience*", who "*live in the passions of the flesh, following the desires of the body and mind*", who are "*by nature the children of wrath*" (Ep 2:1-3), but who also have resolved to find life in Christ.

In other words, if you are a sinner who is trusting Jesus for salvation, then you qualify for every spiritual blessing in the heavenlies!

God did not "*make us alive*" when we were worthy, but when we were "*dead in sins*". He did not raise us up because we deserved such goodness, or had merited it in any way at all, but because "*he is rich in mercy.*" We have not been exalted into the heavenlies because we have a claim upon God's reward, but solely because of "*the great love with which he loved us.*"

But now that we are alive, and raised up, and enthroned with Christ, we are expected to exercise our throne rights and to live victoriously over all the works of Satan.

> *"For we are his workmanship, created in Christ Jesus for good works, which God prepared beforehand, that we should walk in them" (vs.10).*

God did not perform his mighty work of redemption and renewal in us because we were living godly and righteously. The reverse is true. Just because we were dead in sins and totally incapable of doing good, God has quickened us, and raised us, and seated us together with Christ in the heavenlies. We could never have climbed there by ourselves! His grace alone could so exalt us. Faith alone can give us access to these God-created rights.

But now, because we know we are enthroned, because we understand our rights, therefore we can overthrow the deadly grip of sin, treading underfoot every spiritual enemy, and we can victoriously, fruitfully, and happily live before the Lord.

So then, away with that false humility, that spurious servility, that hidden carnal pride, that lustful desire to create one's own goodness, that wicked unbelief that godlessly clings to a position of defeat and of separation from God's blessing.

How dare we say we are not alive when God says we are! How dare we deny the resurrection that God says has happened to us in Christ! How dare we shun our throne rights when God says we are seated with Christ in the heavenlies! How dare we detract from his glorious demonstration throughout "*the coming ages of the immeasurable riches of his grace in kindness toward us in Christ*" by endeavouring to secure his favour on the grounds of our own good works! (vs. 7).

The order is plain. Not good works first, then the throne; but the throne first, then good works. Not overcome sin first, then every spiritual blessing; but first every spiritual blessing, then overcome sin. This is a fact: unless you first grasp "*every spiritual blessing in the heavenlies in Christ*" you will never overcome anything! But when you understand your throne rights, and possess them, and begin to use them, then you will find yourself more than a conqueror through Christ!

Have you ever used a camera that is brought into focus by bringing two images together in its viewfinder? You begin with separate and rather blurred images; you end with one distinct image in sharp focus. Just so, you begin with yourself and Christ separated and out of focus. But as you learn to identify yourself with Christ, bringing yourself together with him by faith, your whole perspective will change. You will see the world from the throne, looking down from the heavenlies. You will no longer be controlled by situational truth, but by positional truth. By the exercise of your throne rights you can change your situation to conform to your true identity and position!

Through your union with Christ by faith, you are a king. So think like a king. Speak like a king. Act like a king. Let nothing deny you your throne rights!

CHAPTER THREE:

COMPLETE AND GLORIOUS

People love to hear secrets, especially when they are someone else's - but you have never heard a more wonderful secret than the one Paul revealed to the church at Colossae. It was a mystery hidden for many generations, one that millions have searched for, and are still searching, but it is now made known to the people of God.

Let Paul give it to you in his own words -

> *"I became a minister according to the divine office that was given to me for you, to make the word of God fully known, the mystery hidden for ages and generations but now made manifest to his saints. To them God chose to make known how great among the Gentiles are the riches of the glory of this mystery, which is Christ in you, the hope of glory" (Col 1:25-28).*

That is not the kind of pronouncement to be greeted with a yawn. It is startling! It is arresting! It speaks about "*riches*" and "*glory*" and "*revelation*"!

Here is a mystery unravelled. Here is a treasure exposed. Here is a miracle inwrought. Here is one of the most superb statements in the entire Bible: "*Christ is in you, the hope of glory.*"

RICHES BEYOND ALL TELLING

THE MYSTERY REVEALED

Are you a Christian? Has the new birth been wrought in you by the Holy Spirit? Have you been brought into union with Christ by faith? Then look at yourself, and say boldly: "*Christ is in <u>me</u>, the hope of glory!*"

No one in the old dispensation ever imagined that this was God's amazing plan. No one ever dared to think that the Messiah, when he came, would find his chief glory in union with each one of his people. Yes, with each one of them! For it does not say that "*Christ is in the good, the hope of glory*". Nor does it deny that he is in the bad. Rather, whoever is a true member of the church which is his body is included in the affirmation, "*Christ is in you!*"

Not all members of the true church live godly and victoriously. Some of them are bothered by sin, defeated by habit, plagued by doubt, troubled by fear. But none of them is excluded from the great mystery now revealed to the saints: Christ, the hope of glory, is in each one of them.

Now this means that every believer has come into a relationship with God through Christ which is deeper, more vital, than any other relationship. It surpasses the union between husband and wife, or parent and child. It is deeper than that between brothers or sisters. It goes far beyond the bond of friendship. This is no mere business association, nor even one based on social or spiritual affinity. Rather, it is a consanguineous relationship as close as that which inheres between my soul and my spirit.

Paul is bold enough to say that "*we are members of his body, of his flesh, and of his bones*" (Ep 5:30, AV). And Jesus himself expressed a similar idea when he solemnly declared: "*Truly, truly, I say to you, unless you eat the flesh of the Son of man and drink his blood, you have no life in you ... He who eats my flesh and drinks my blood abides in me, and I in him*" (Jn 6:53- 55).

What remarkable words: "*bone of his bone, flesh of his flesh*"! How astonishing to hear Jesus talking about us "*eating his flesh and drinking his blood*"!

It is difficult not to be offended by such expressions.

What do they mean?

Christ himself explained that he did not intend his words to be understood crudely and physically. But he did mean them to be taken literally, in the sense that they describe the strength and totality of the union with him which becomes ours through faith.

That union is as deep, as infusive, as if our flesh and bones had become amalgamated with his, or as though we had indeed eaten his flesh or drunk his blood. But he makes it clear that this is really a spiritual union that results from our faith in him:

> *"Truly, truly, I say to you, he who believes has eternal life ... It is the spirit that gives life, the flesh is of no avail; the words that I have spoken to you are spirit and life. But there are some of you that do not believe" (vs. 47,63,64).*

Truly, this is a mystery: that I, a child of time, should be linked with the Father of eternity, and that earth should be joined with heaven, corruption with in-corruption, evil with good, guilt with innocence, the unholy with the holy, and the weak with the strong!

But scripture declares it, and you and I are called on to believe it! Christ is in me! A divine amalgam has occurred. The hope of glory indwells every believer. We have come into an ineffable union with the Son of God.

What are the ramifications of this splendid mystery, now revealed, that "*Christ is in me*"?

THE MYSTERY EXPLAINED

As he attempts to reveal all of the wonder and promise of this great union between Christ and the believer, Paul uses three nouns that are pregnant with power: "*riches ... glory ... hope.*"

1 - THERE ARE "RICHES" IN THIS MYSTERY

Incalculable wealth is in the hands of those who are in Christ's hand!

There are riches of pardon:

- for this Christ who is in you is more vast than all of your sin; his righteousness swallows your iniquity as the ocean swallows a cupful of ink. He indwells you, not as judge and tormentor, but as the source of all mercy, the fountain of all life.

When you boldly affirm, "*Christ is in me!*" you are in fact confessing that the holiness of God is in you, and that no voice of condemnation can be effectively raised against you (Ro 8:1).

The sin that is interwoven with every fibre of our being, which stains our every thought, word, and deed, and which turns even our seemingly good actions into menstrual rags (Is 64:6), is utterly erased by the invincible purity of this indwelling Christ.

Without him we are inescapably guilty; with him we are irresistibly innocent!

There are riches of healing:

- for the life of Christ in us has power to consume death and its harbinger, disease. Paul shouted with joy,
- *"The law of the Spirit of life in Christ Jesus has set me free from the law of sin and death" (Ro 8:2).*
- This law of life functions in every believer. It is in your voice when you pray, in your spirit when you worship, in your mind when you meditate, in your hands when you lay them on the sick in Jesus' name. The Christ who is in you is the Great Physician, the Vanquisher of death, the Resurrection and the Life, Yahweh-Rapha, the Source of all healing.

If you can believe it, "*the law of the Spirit of life*" in you is a law of healing. You can tap into this law and cause it to act as divine medicine for every illness. You can also join this law with the use of ordinary medicines and expect some extraordinary results!

There are riches of fellowship:

for by the indwelling Christ we are brought into profound union with God. The Father can no longer be thought of as absent or abstract. In the reality of my affirmation, "Christ is in me!" God himself is made wonderfully real, and an awareness is born that nothing save unbelief can ever separate me from the love of the Father.

There are riches of strength:

> *- for if you know that "**Christ is in you, the hope of glory**", how could you ever again feel inadequate for any task God may give you, or for any situation into which he may lead you? You can do everything through the strength of Christ! (Ph 4:13).*
>
> *You are "strengthened with all might, according to Christ's glorious might, for all endurance and patience with joy" (Col 1:11).*
>
> *The greatness of the power working in us who believe is immeasurable, for it is the working of the incomparable might of the risen Christ! (Ep 1:19-20).*

If Christ is in you, that strength is in you, to make you at all times "*more than a conqueror*"! (Ro 8:37).

2 - THERE IS GLORY IN THIS MYSTERY

The Greek word is "*doxa*", and no single English word is a suitable equivalent. The basic meaning of "*doxa*" is an opinion, an evaluation, an assessment of the worth of something, whether this assessment is true or false. So something might seem to you to be either beautiful or base, but in either case "*doxa*" could be used to describe your opinion.

However, in the Greek world "*doxa*" most commonly referred to a good opinion of something (or of someone), and it was frequently extended to describe the honour, praise, or reward that resulted from being well spoken of. Hence it was focussed again to describe the special dignity and advantage that would come to those whom God deemed worthy.

Hence in the NT the "*glorification*" (*doxa*) of the saints includes the ideas of future bliss, of being invested with dazzling radiance and clothed with magnificence, of obtaining the lustre of royalty, full of majesty and dignity, of sharing in the beauty, wealth, and excellencies of the kingdom of heaven.

But all of that begins with the good opinion God has of those whom he beholds only through his Son. If you can faithfully affirm "*Christ is in me!*" then God has only one notion concerning you: to honour you by a good report and to array you with all of the splendour of his kingdom (cp. Mt 13:43).

Admittedly, it is possible to nullify God's report by grieving the Holy Spirit through wilful and continuous sin. There is a kind of sin that despises the righteous covenant, destroys the efficacy of Christ, and arouses the anger of God (Ep 4:30; He 10:26-31).

But "although I speak like this, beloved, I am sure that what I am saying does not apply to you; for you are capable of better things, and you are on the way to full salvation" (6:9, paraphrased). The fact is, no-one who understands that Christ has come into union with every believer, and who confidently and joyfully cries, "Christ in me is the end of sin," can go right on sinning! That affirmation is designed to destroy sin, not to enhance it. Those who want to sin will not open their mouths to testify that Christ is in them. Even if, out of habit or circumstance, they do mouth the words, they will be speaking in unbelief, not faith.

But I am supposing that your desire is toward righteousness, not unrighteousness. And if that is so, then even if temptation does overtake you and sin snares you from time to time, you can still say, through laughter and tears, "*Christ is still in me, the hope of glory!*"

The devil, and your own conscience, may speak ill of you, but God, for Christ's sake, speaks well of you. His "*doxa*" is conveyed to you. You become a possessor of the beauty and dignity of holiness - not in yourself, but in Christ.

Now if God sees you as "*glorious*" you should see yourself so. No longer look upon yourself as the grovelling slave of sin and of eternal judgment, but rather see yourself standing tall in the freedom and self-mastery that are yours in Christ.

I have indicated in another place[4] that there is a kind of spurious piety that is never happy unless it is miserable. Deeply suspicious of cheerfulness (which they deem frivolity), and of optimism (which they deem presumption), these masochistic Christians endlessly flagellate themselves with self-recrimination. They cannot resist the urge to thrash themselves with piteous protestations of unworthiness.

No doubt their low opinion of themselves is well deserved, but it hardly pleases God to hear them say it over and over again. He would rather hear them extol the merits of his Son! In place of endless admissions of defeat he would prefer to hear a bold faith-confession of victory in Christ.

But the many modern exponents of the miseries of the medieval hermits are determined to stay bowed by their self-inflicted chains; they have never learned the faith of the man who sings "*Yea, by thee I can crush a troop; and by my God I can leap over a wall!*" (Ps 18:29).

If you happen to sin, you should certainly repent sorrowfully and at once confess your sin to the Father. But as soon as you have acknowledged your fault, you should confidently appropriate the pardon and purification God offers you in Christ, and never mention that sin again, unless as a basis of praise for God's wonderful mercy and grace!

---

[4] See the DCC course on "Christian Life."

And the moment your sin is placed under the blood of the cross you should begin again to speak as well of yourself in Christ as God does. Despite that now forgiven and forgotten sin (He 8:12), Christ in you is still glorious, and you are still glorious in Christ.

This "*glory*" is a restoration of your dignity; it is the favourable opinion God has concerning you in Christ; it is the marvellous inheritance prepared for you in the heavenlies; it is the breathtaking effulgence that will clothe you on the day of resurrection. And it is in you now, in Christ, waiting to be appreciated and appropriated by faith.

3 - THERE IS "HOPE" IN THIS MYSTERY

"*Hope*" in the world and "*hope*" in the kingdom of God are not the same thing. In the world, "*hope*" always contains an element of uncertainty - "*I hope Sam will come (but I am not sure).*" But in the kingdom of God that uncertainty is removed. He who hopes in God possesses confidence; his hope is unchanging and eternal -

> *"God wanted to make it very clear to those who were to receive what he promised that he would never change his purpose; so he added his vow to the promise. There are two things, then, that cannot change and about which God cannot lie. So we who have found safety with him are greatly encouraged to hold firmly to the hope that is placed before us. We have this hope as an anchor for our hearts. It is safe and sure, and goes through the curtain of the heavenly temple into the inner sanctuary" (He 6:17-19, GNB).*

Our hope is secured by two things: God's promise, and God's sworn oath to keep his promise. The vow and the promise are both immutable. God cannot lie. What he has spoken he will perform. Thus we have a safe and sure hope, one in which our souls may take calm refuge.

This hope of ours embraces many things, but they can all be summed up in two words -

RESURRECTION

If Christ, the Lord of life, is joined to me by an indestructible bond, then I cannot die. Death becomes only a momentary transition from time into eternity, and from the trammels of the flesh into the limitless freedom of an immortal son of God.

Jesus said: "*I am the resurrection and the life; he who believes in me, though he die, yet shall he live, <u>and whoever lives and believes in me shall never die</u>*" (Jn 11:25-26). We die, yet we do not die. Death for us is changed. Its sting is drawn. By the Christ who is in me, the death that worked in me so remorselessly is now made innocuous. His life is stronger than death.

If I should die, it will not be because of the working of sin, but because of the working of God. Formerly my dying was contrary to his will. It was the savage outworking of his broken law, the penalty for my own transgressions and for those of my forebears. But now my dying is pleasant in his sight. It is to him a precious event; for it is his gracious will that by this process I shall escape the world and enter into all of the joy of my Lord. And all of this takes place in union with Christ. Nothing before the grave, in the grave, nor after the grave, can alter that blessed mystery: "*Christ is in me, the hope of glory!*"

INHERITANCE

If we are the children of God, and if Christ is in us by an indissoluble union, then it inescapably follows that we are "*heirs of God and fellow heirs with Christ*" (Ro 8:17).

To be a "*fellow heir*" means to have an equal inheritance: that is, to have the same right of inheritance that he has.

Just as my wife and I are joint owners of the house in which we live (which means, not that we each own half of the house, but that we both own the whole house), so Christ, through his union with me, has brought me to a full share of the kingdom of God. Of all that he is heir to, we who believe in him are also inheritors.

This inheritance may include his sufferings, as Paul goes on to say, but it certainly includes his glory - that is, the right to sit upon his throne and to possess the splendours of his kingdom.

THE MYSTERY APPLIED

In the application of this great "*mystery*" there are two things: warning, and opportunity.

There is a warning to remember that you can be presented to God in glory only by virtue of union with Christ.

If you try to stand before God by yourself, without Christ, depending on your own merits rather than his, you will utterly fail.

We have hope of glory only because we can affirm, "*Christ is in me!*" No other affirmation has any value, no other is necessary. If I am truly united with Christ then he has become all my hope, my only source of "*wisdom, righteousness, sanctification, and redemption.*"

> *I am content to be accepted solely in the Beloved. If I boast at all, my boast shall be in him! (1 Co 1:30-31; Ep 1:6).*

There is also an opportunity, now that the secret has been revealed to us through the gospel, to hear the good news, to personalise it, to believe it, to experience it in life.

God is no longer absent or abstract! His life and your life are intertwined through Christ. The things you feel, he feels; if you rejoice, he laughs with you; if you weep, your sorrow touches him. He shares! He cares! Those who harm you harm "*the apple of his eye*" (Zc 2:8).

So then, you must reciprocate the good word God has spoken to you in Christ by personalising the promise for yourself. That is, think of it, speak of it, as a thing that is wonderfully real to you (not merely a nice theory).

Declare it with passion and joy: "*Christ is in me, the hope of glory!*" Begin living in the fact that you are indeed united with Christ; let this marvellous mystery (now revealed) be the reference point for all of your thinking and believing; let it be the force that daily transforms you into the radiant beauty of Christ himself.

COMPLETE IN CHRIST

See Col 2:8-10.

The clause that should arrest your attention is in verse 10: "*You have come to fullness of life in him.*"

That is an extraordinary statement. Translators have difficulty conveying its full meaning in English, as the following excerpts will show -

> *"You have been given full life in union with him" (GNB)*
>
> *"You have everything when you have Christ" (Taylor)*
>
> *"Your own completeness is realised in him" (Phillips)*
>
> *"In him you too find your own fulfilment" (Jerusalem)*

But in this instance I like best of all the Authorised Version: "*Ye are complete in him, which is the head of all principality and power.*"

"Complete!"

There could hardly be a more concrete or absolute word! No lack, no shortage, no emptiness, no inadequacy. Just complete!

The Greek noun is "*pleroma*", and with astonishing boldness Paul applies it first to Christ, and then, in the very next sentence, to us -

> *"In Christ all the pleroma of the Godhead dwells bodily" ... and ...*
>
> *"You have come to pleroma of life in Christ."*[5]

If the fullness of God truly dwells in Christ, then the fullness of Christ truly dwells in us. If Christ is complete in God, then we are complete in Christ. Just as Jesus was able to declare, "*The Father is in me, and I am in the Father,*" so you can positively confess, "*Christ is in me, and I am in Christ*" (Jn. 10:38). Just as Christ was full of the Father, so every believer is full of Christ (Col. 1:27; Jn. 17:23; 14:20; Ep. 3:17).

To be indwelt by Christ in this way is to be complete. It is to have everything you need to fulfil the purpose of God for your life and to realise the full potential of every ability God has given you. It is to have within yourself a source of supply which makes you fully able to cope with every situation in life. It is the state superlatively described by Paul -

> *"God is able to provide you with every blessing in abundance, so that you may always have enough of everything and may provide in abundance for every good work" (2 Co 9:8).*

This is an exciting promise indeed! Let us discover God's riches here ...

THE MEANING OF "PLEROMA"

Possibly the best literal translation of "*pleroma*" would be "*filled full*". Indeed, the Greek word has been adopted into our language, almost with that very sense. According to my dictionary, "*pleroma*" describes "*a state of overflowing abundance,*" and it is

[5] Verses 9,10. The form in vs.10 is actually that of a participle, perfect tense, passive voice.

used when no ordinary English word can be found to describe extraordinary richness. It conjures an image of extravagant provision, of enormous surplus.

This idea of "*fullness*" is conveyed by the use of the word in the NT:

> "<u>To cram with abundance</u>" - "when it was full (pleroma)" (Mt 13:48).
>
> "To level up every low place" (Lu 3:5).
>
> "<u>To pervade every part</u>" (Jn 12:3; Ac 2:2).
>
> "<u>To make replete</u>" - "I have all, and abound, I am full (pleroma) ... My God will fulfil (pleroma) every need of yours" (Ph 4:18-19).

Notice the homeliness of "*I'm full!*" - the expression of a man who has eaten too much! It describes an over-sufficient satisfaction, deep contentment, a state of having more-than-enough. As the Philippians had so bountifully provided for Paul (vs. 14-18), so in turn he promises that God will provide for them. Likewise, the supply God gives us in Christ is more than enough to make up every deficiency, to satisfy every emptiness, to complete every need.

Putting those definitions together, "*pleroma*" conveys the idea of being "*filled full*" of God - to the point of total satisfaction, of overflowing with the wealth of his blessings, of having every hollow become a mountain, of being permeated by God in every part of one's being.

The expression "*filled full*" might seem to be a tautology. But it is a fact that something can be full, yet not full. Take a bucket and fill it with tennis balls. It is full, yet it is not full, for you can still place a great many ball-bearings in the same bucket. Even then it is not yet completely full, for there is still room for a quantity of sand; and even after this, the bucket can be filled again with water. It might then be said to be filled-full, crammed, replete, with room for nothing else!

That is the sense of Paul's words in Ep 1:3 - "Blessed be the God and Father of our Lord Jesus Christ, who has blessed us in Christ with every spiritual blessing."

And it is worth noting again that in this verse, as well as in our text (Col 2:10), the verb is in the past tense. It is a statement of fact. God has already blessed us with every spiritual blessing; we are even now complete in Christ.

But if it is true that all blessing, authority, provision, fullness, victory, healing, freedom, and so on, are already the full possession of every believer, how is it that so many apparently suffer from an almost total lack of those things?

HOW TO ENJOY "PLEROMA" IN CHRIST

This "*completeness*", like every other aspect of the gospel, becomes real in a person's life only in conjunction with three other things

- it is available in Christ alone.
- it must be embraced by faith.
- it must be released by confession.

If you are a Christian, a "*born again*" believer, then you are spiritually complete in Christ and potentially complete in experience. But this potential experience of fullness of life in Christ can explode into reality only when it is triggered by a bold faith-confession. You will not actually become "*complete*" until you deeply believe that in Christ you are in fact already "*complete*"; and when you believe it you will irresistibly speak it (Mt 12:34b).

Hear it. Believe it. Speak it. That is the three-fold faith formula that activates the promise of God!

You are certainly not "*complete*" in yourself. On the contrary, you are doubtless aware of areas in your life where you are defeated, or diseased, or deficient. But the challenge of scripture is not to measure yourself by yourself, but by Christ. In him you are complete. You have come to fullness of life

> spiritually: for you are now reconciled to God and brought into perfect fellowship with the Father, having received eternal life and been made a member of his body on earth, the church.
>
> mentally: for although your mind was once enveloped in darkness, you are now able to comprehend spiritual things, to know the truth and to discover freedom in Christ (Jn 8:32,36).
>
> morally: for you once lacked the knowledge of God's will, and were void of any dynamic that could have enabled you to observe his law; but now you are able to be clothed with power by his Spirit and to live in harmony with his law.
>
> physically: for you were once a slave to disease and death, but now a remedy for disease has been freely provided by the Great Physician, and death has become merely the doorway to endless Life!

Your affirmation of those things will make them real in your daily experience.

Suppose you have sinned?

What will your confession be? One of despairing defeat? Will you fall to denigrating yourself, castigating your weakness, bemoaning your unworthiness, calling yourself a miserable failure, an unhappy wretch, and so on?

If you behave in that fashion you will succeed only in strengthening the grip that sin already has on you - for there is no surer way to increase your bondage to some habit or personal failure than to make it the subject of most of your thinking, talking, and praying.

But if, having once confessed your defeat and sought the pardon of God, you then turn your attention fully to the perfection of Christ, and begin again, joyfully, continually, and aggressively, to declare yourself complete in him, then you will actually experience more and more of his righteousness.

You cannot create righteousness by concentrating on sin.

If you want to become like Christ then you must focus attention on his excellencies, and think, pray, and talk about his glory. The more you rejoice in the victory of Christ, and the more you praise God for making you a participant in that victory, the more that victory will be enacted in your own experience.

When should you begin to make that faith-confession? Plainly, right now, whether or not you are still outwardly defeated!

Remember, you are praising God for what you are in Christ, and this has nothing to do with what you are in yourself. But such praise will irresistibly change what you are in yourself to what you are in Christ!

Suppose you are sick, will your conversation, your prayers, your believing, be engrossed with the symptoms and distress of your illness? Or will you turn your attention away from your physical condition, and instead emphasise the declaration of scripture that you are "*complete*" in Christ?

Perpetual confession of sickness will increase its virulence; but confession of the good health God has promised you in Christ will open the door to recovery.

The fact of the believer's completeness in Christ cannot change. It remains as true as the eternal Christ himself. The Christ in me is complete, and I am complete in him. That is a word spoken by God, and it is not dependent for its truth upon any outward circumstance. It expresses a spiritual reality, effective for every Christian.

Our part is to accept what God says and thank him for it. Let God be true and everything else a lie! If scripture says that you are now blessed with every spiritual blessing, then believe that good word, and rejoice in it. If it says that you are more than a conqueror, that you are healed, that you have authority over Satan, that you are holy, unblameable, unreprovable, and so on, then trust God's testimony and be glad! Do not be governed by the evidence of your senses, nor of your circumstances, but determine to accept and to confess only what God says.

He says that in Christ you are complete, spiritually, mentally, morally, physically. Your joyful affirmation of God's word to you in Christ, despite any outward evidence, will create a faith channel through which the law of the Spirit of life can work to make you whole.

REIGNING IN LIFE

Have you heard the expression "*king for a day*"? It refers to a custom practised by several countries in the past of raising a slave to the throne for just one day. For a few hours the slave became a ruler, and the rulers slaves. However, the peasant "*king*" had to be wary how he used his new-found authority, for his tenure of the throne was short and any abuse of power would be swiftly avenged.

God has done something far greater for us. We were slaves. But he has now elevated us to his throne, in Christ, not just for a day, but for ever! This is Paul's theme when he exults: "

> *We who have received abundance of grace and the free gift of righteousness, shall reign in life through Jesus Christ" (Ro 5:17).*

There are some exciting things to explore here -

BY ONE MAN WE DIE
BY ONE MAN WE LIVE

See Ro 5:12-17, which discusses the origin of the sin and death that all men share in common, and describes God's magnificent solution in Christ.

Paul begins with the statement, "*Sin came into the world through one man and death through sin, and so death spread to all men because all men sinned.*" He then goes on to develop the idea that through our natural birth, and the sin that inevitably accompanies human life, we all share in Adam's death. But God has wrought more mightily than death, so that now, by the new birth, he has given us eternal life. Death came by one man, Adam; life comes by another man, Christ.

Paul then draws a contrast between the results of Adam's trespass and the results of God's free grace. In the case of Adam, the one trespass of the one man brought death to many, followed by the judgment and condemnation of God (vs. 12-14).

But in the case of Christ, the effect of God's free gift "is not like the effect of (Adam's) sin"; for despite the many sins of many people,

> *"the grace of God and the free gift that came by the grace of that one man Jesus Christ has abounded for many" (vs. 15-16).*

Now the important thing here is that just as one man was sufficient to bring death upon us all, so one man is sufficient to bring life. Furthermore, we received death from Adam as a free gift, whether we wanted it or not. Being born into the Adamic race we inevitably share its heritage of death. But likewise, Christ, "the last Adam," offers his righteousness, and eternal life, as a free gift to all who believe. This divine life is an integral part of the new birth wrought in us by the Holy Spirit.

Those who are born of the race of Adam possess defeat and death; but those who are born of the new creation in Christ possess victory and life -

> *"Just as one man's trespass led to condemnation for all men, so one man's act of righteousness leads to acquittal and life for all men. For as by one man's disobedience many were made sinners, so by one man's obedience many will be made righteous ... so that, as sin reigned in death, grace also might reign through righteousness to eternal life through Jesus Christ our Lord" (vs. 18-21).*

The reign of sin has been supplanted by the reign of grace. The one expressed itself through the "free gift" of condemnation and death; the other is manifested in the "free gift" of righteousness and life.

To receive Adam's gift it is necessary only to remain a member of his race. To receive Christ's gift it is necessary only to enter his new creation!

Now if grace is reigning in us then

WE ARE CALLED TO REIGN IN LIFE

Nine times in this one passage of scripture Paul uses the superlative "*polus*" = "*much*" - vs. 9,10,15 (thrice), 16,17,19 (twice). He is talking about abounding sin, and even more abounding grace, and he stretches the limits of language as he tries to convey the magnitude of the death sin brought and the greater magnitude of the life grace brings. "*Polus*" might be translated as "*much more*" or "*the many*":

- "much more shall we be saved by Christ" (vs. 9)
- "much more shall we be saved by his life" (vs. 10)
- "the many died through one man's trespass" (vs. 15)
- "much more has the grace of God abounded for the many" (vs. 15)

- "the free gift following <u>many</u> trespasses brings justification" (vs. 16)
- "<u>much more</u> will we reign in life through Christ" (vs. 17)
- "<u>the many</u> were made sinners, <u>the many</u> will be made righteousness" (vs. 19)

I want to concentrate on "*the much more*" of God's grace to us in Christ ...

(1) THE "MUCH MORE" OF OUR SALVATION (VS. 9,10)

Paul presents together two great aspects of the work of Christ: his death and his resurrection. Then he adds the two-fold benefit that has now accrued to us: total escape from the wrath of God; and full access to his life and fellowship.

By the atoning death of Jesus we gained a legal acquittal from all charges of violating God's law - "*we are now justified by his blood.*" But if Christ has so made atonement for sin will he now leave us defenceless in the day of judgment? Hardly, says Paul. We can be sure that having secured our legal right to pardon, Christ will in that day "*much more save us from the wrath of God.*"

But Paul is not satisfied to rest there. He is not content with a salvation that offers only a right to acquittal in the day of judgment. He wants to experience the grace of God in this present life. And he discovers that this is also part of the gospel - for did not Christ love us, and die for us, and reconcile us to God while we were still enemies of God? But if his death could achieve such a wonderful reconciliation while we were still his enemies, how much more will his life achieve for us now that we are his friends!

Therefore Paul writes: "For if while we were enemies we were reconciled to God by the death of his Son, much more, now that we are reconciled, we shall be saved by his life!" (vs. 10).

So the death of Christ gives us access to the legal pardon of God; but the resurrection of Christ gives us access to the living power of God.

If Christ is alive in us, then we are alive in Christ! And this life in us is indestructible. It cannot die as did the life of Adam. If we die in the flesh, it is Adamic life that dies. But the life of Christ within us lives on, and we too live in that life (Jn 11:25-26).

Death could not chain Jesus, nor could the grave imprison him. Nothing could withstand him as he rolled away the stone and walked out of the tomb. But now this irresistible resurrection life is surging within every person who comes into union with Christ through faith. Paul says "we shall be saved by his life" - and he means today as well as tomorrow.

The word "*saved*" = "*sozo*", and it describes complete salvation of body, soul, and spirit. It means to rescue spiritually and physically. It refers to both spiritual and bodily healing. It includes deliverance from any kind of personal bondage and freedom from every affliction of Satan. So when Paul says "*we are saved by his life*" he must be understood as saying also "*we are healed by his life*" or "*delivered by his life*" or "*preserved unharmed by his life.*"[6]

But the effectiveness of this great salvation can be nullified by unbelief. You can refuse to admit that the resurrection life of Christ is at work within you. You can refuse to shake off your chains and step out of your prison. You can close your lips and refuse to shout "*I am being saved by his life!*" In that case, sin will continue to bind your soul, and disease will maintain its grip on your flesh.

But if you boldly take hold of God's "*much more*", knowing it belongs to you, knowing that you stand in the grace of God, and that you have obtained access to the fullness of Christ, then you will rejoice in the hope of sharing in his glory and of his resurrection life making you whole! (vs. 2).

---

[6] There is a more detailed study of "*sozo*" in the book, "**Healing In The Whole Bible**."

(2) THE "MUCH MORE" OF OUR PERSONAL VICTORY (VS.17)

As people who are indwelt by the living Christ, we are called to "*reign in life*", that is, not to be defeated, but to be victorious in every situation.

It is impossible for the Christ who is in you ever to be defeated. For that reason, so long as you remain united with him through faith, it is ultimately impossible for you to be defeated.

There simply is no defeat for the people of God.

Even when they lose, they win, so long as Christ is in them! Their death becomes resurrection, their sin is drowned in the grace of God, their failures are stepping stones to a greater success!

Concerning the conflict of the saints with Satan the Bible has only three words to say: "*they overcame him*" (Re 12:11). Not once does it say, "*they were overcome by him.*" They may lose a battle, perhaps many battles, but the saints will inevitably win the war!

They can be knocked down but never knocked out!

The reason is simple. The weapons they use are those that unite them with Christ, and in alliance with him it is utterly impossible for them to be finally overcome by the world or by Satan. Those weapons are, "*the blood of the Lamb, and the word of their testimony.*" If you believe in your heart that Jesus died for your sins, if you confess him with your mouth as Lord, knowing that he is alive from the dead, then you possess those weapons. By them you come into full union with Christ. His invincibility becomes yours. To destroy you, Satan would first have to destroy the Christ who is in you, and that he cannot ever do.

So if you are in Christ, you are a person who ultimately cannot possibly be defeated. No weapon that is forged against you can ever finally prosper (Is 54:17). Your enemy may succeed for a time, but eventually he will fall and you will irresistibly and totally prevail against him. Your word will be that of Micah: "*Rejoice not over me, O my enemy; when I fall, I shall rise; when I sit in darkness, the Lord will be a light to me ... He will bring me forth to the light; I shall behold his deliverance. Then my enemy will see (and be ashamed)*" (7:8-10).

But there is no reason for this victory over Satan and circumstance to be entirely reserved for the future. Since you must eventually triumph, why not start conquering now? Since you must eventually reign, why not reign now? Since you know that you are really unconquerable, why not impose that victory upon your enemy now?

There was a time when one man's sin caused death to reign over me (Ro 5:17); and along with death came all manner of personal defeat, illness, and fear. But if Adam's sin had power to make me a slave, how much more does Christ's obedience have power to make me a king!

> *"If, because of one man's trespass, death reigned through that one man, much more will those who receive the abundance of grace and the free gift of righteousness reign in life through the one man Jesus Christ."*

In this present life I was made a slave to sin and death; in this present life I can reign in righteousness. Knowing that I have access to abundance of grace in Christ, I can never tolerate any kind of defeat. My goal must be to enjoy in all its fullness the "*much more*" of the personal victory God has given me - a victory immensely greater than any enemy has ever gained over me.

Now if we do have in Christ a victory "*much more*" potent than our former defeat, and if we have truly received "*abundance of grace*", and if we are really called to "*reign in life*", then it follows that there are only two approaches we should take in any situation:

- change it by faith, or
- control it by faith.

Those are the only modes of action approved by God. He certainly does not condone a defeatist attitude. He does not allow that his people should be mere victims of circumstance, driven here and there, completely at the mercy of whatever happens (cp. Ja 1:5-8). He calls them to rule their circumstances, not be ruled by them.

I do not mean that nothing should ever happen that is beyond your physical control. That would be foolish. Many events occur that we cannot alter. Peter, for example, was warned by Jesus,

> *"Truly, truly, I say to you, when you were young, you girded yourself and walked where you would; but when you are old, you will stretch out your hands, and another will gird you and carry you where you do not wish to go" (Jn 21:18).*

And John adds,

> *"Jesus said this to show Peter by what death he was to glorify God."*

Even Jesus himself would fain have avoided the cross if the Father had permitted it.

Some happenings we cannot prevent nor avoid.

But we can maintain inner mastery, no matter what is occurring in the world around us.

Yet there are other times when God is willing to grant his children faith for a miracle that may shake the earth and change the course of history. Either to control each circumstance, or to change it - faith will always find scope to do one or the other.

For example, do you remember the night when the disciples were sent by Jesus to cross the lake in a fishing boat?

At midnight a terrible storm sprang up, and the disciples were overwhelmed with horror as they felt their boat sinking. They were captured by the storm. It had shattered their faith, and they were entirely at its mercy.

But Jesus came walking toward them across the water. The disciples were so victimised by the storm, they failed to recognise him, and, thinking he was an evil spectre, they cried out in still greater terror.

But Christ was in full mastery of himself and of the storm. The wind and waves howled around him, but he walked calmly on. Here is faith exercising control over the circumstance.

Later, when he had joined the disciples in their boat and had banished their fear, Jesus acted more strongly and commanded the storm to be still. Immediately a wonderful peace covered the whole lake.

Here is faith changing the circumstance.

At the end of his life, when those murderers took him and brutally crucified him, Jesus was still the master. He had yielded himself to the will of God, and hence to their wicked hands - but he remained in control of his own spirit, and he triumphed over all of the uglincss of Golgotha. He controlled the cross, it did not control him. It was not able to make him a mere victim, helpless before hatred and violence.

But then once more, by faith he acted not merely to control but to change, when he forced asunder the bars of death and rose victoriously out of the grave.

In every circumstance in life God challenges us also to act in faith, either to control or to change the things that are happening. Men may bind your hands and your feet, they may rob you of your possessions, they may threaten your life; or chance or accident may overshadow you with disaster; or you may find yourself imprisoned by stone walls and iron bars, which no hand can break; but within that prison, or under that shadow, or despite that persecution, you can call upon God and get a word from him that will enable you to gloriously "*reign in life*"!

Perhaps by faith he will enable you to triumph magnificently in your spirit so that even crucifixion will become redemption and a marvellous crown. Or he may give you a word of faith that will enable you to move mountains, wrench the prison doors open, call down fire from heaven, and create a stupendous miracle of deliverance.

Thus Paul and Silas were not subdued by the cruel Roman lash, nor by the wrenching anguish of the stocks, nor by the cold strength of their prison walls. They showed that they were still free men, in control of the situation, when at midnight they sang boisterously the praises of God. This was faith exercising mastery within every circumstance, whether or not those circumstances were changed.

In the case of those two apostles, however, God resolved to do more. So he acted in response to their praise and tore the prison apart by a great earthquake. This was faith causing a miracle which actually changed the circumstances.

But it is worth noting that Paul and Silas were free men before the earthquake loosed their chains and the jailer sent them away. They were just as free inside the prison as they were outside it. Their freedom lay within themselves. It was the freedom of faith, the triumph of men in Christ who had learned how to "*reign in life*".

(3) THE "MUCH MORE" OF OUR FUTURE DESTINY (VS. 21)

Once the whole earth was overlorded by sin and death, but God determined that sin should never be mightier than his grace. Hence "*where sin abounded, grace abounded all the more, so that, as sin reigned in death, grace also might reign through righteousness to eternal life through Jesus Christ our Lord.*"

Our destiny in Christ is to inherit eternal life. This is not a life (such as that possessed by Adam) that can be lost. It is as endless as God himself. Whoever has this life lives for ever, and this life brings with it possession of the kingdom of God and a seat upon the throne of God.

But whoever lives in the kingdom of God also reigns there! Such is your destiny, and mine, if we cling firmly to Christ.

Within that kingdom there are no doubt degrees of authority and of sovereignty, and not all of the saints will obtain the same reward; but they are all nonetheless "*a nation of kings and priests*" (1 Pe 2:9; Ex 19:6), and they will all one day reign with Christ - "*some over ten cities some over five*", and so on (cp. Lu 19:11-26).

This greater glory still lies ahead of us; but as members of God's royal priesthood, every believer is able right now "to be enlightened, to taste the heavenly gift, to become partakers of the Holy Spirit, and to taste the goodness of the word of God and the powers of the age to come" (He 6:4-5).

We have access now to the inheritance laid up for us in the future. We can today "*taste*" something of the coming heavenly gift, and we can grasp some measure of "the powers" of that mighty kingdom of God.

You who will reign upon the throne then can actually reign in life now!

Adam had a kingdom and lost it. But God has restored to us "*much more*" than our ancestor forfeited. His was an earthly paradise alone. But our inheritance embraces the span not only of the present world but also the coming new earth and new heaven - it reaches from time into eternity!

What are the "*powers*" of this coming age that the apostle says we can already experience in this one?

The word is *dunamis*, which means basically "*power, strength, ability, energy*", and by extension "*a miracle*", or "*a mighty work*". Dunamis is used frequently with all of those meanings in the NT.

So then, to "*taste the powers of the coming kingdom of God*" means: to have access to all of the energy of that coming divine kingdom; to share now in its mighty works of healing and deliverance; to experience its wonderful dynamic; to draw on its strength and power; to enjoy its profuse supply, its wealth and plenty, whether materially or spiritually.

We who are children of the kingdom can have a foretaste now, a kind of preview, of the splendour and glory of that magnificent future age!

How to do that will be the opening theme of the next chapter.

CHAPTER FOUR:

HIDDEN WITH CHRIST

The previous chapter ended with the exciting idea that we who are united with Christ by faith can already, in this present life, experience "*the powers of the coming age*" (He 6:5). We saw also that this is part of what it means to reign in life through Christ (Ro 5:17).

We take up that theme again, and learn that there are four keys to the discovery of this royal mastery

HOW TO REIGN IN LIFE

CHOICE

You will not begin to reign over life until you choose to do so. The Holy Spirit is moving you to resolve right now to live like the king God has called you to be. The throne of authority, of victory, of healing, of supply, is waiting for you to step up to, and to be seated on it.

God has done his part in Christ. It now remains for you to decide whether you will adopt the stance of a serf or a sovereign. You can place yourself upon the throne and begin to reign in life, in the name of Jesus; or you can abdicate your royal authority, and continue living as though Christ has not risen from the dead, as though the Holy Spirit has not been given to you, and as though the resurrection life of Jesus is not filling you.

When you choose to reign like a king, then you will begin to live like one!

CONFIDENCE

Let no doubts keep you away from this wonderful privilege of reigning in life. God gives you a place on his throne, not because of any worthiness of yours, but solely because of the merits of Christ. You may indeed begin reigning in life - yet not in your own name, but only in the name of Jesus. The entire work springs out of his "*abundance of grace*" (Ro 5:17).

Therefore, no good work you can do will give you any better access to the throne than you gain immediately by faith in Jesus' name. On the contrary, if you presume to place God in your debt by good works you may arouse his anger and cause him to act against you instead of for you.

If I have stressed any idea in these chapters it is surely this: no favour from God can be bought or earned. There is room only for grace. Nothing can be received except what is already freely available through faith in Christ. The message of scripture remains each day the same: whatever the circumstances may be, any child of God may at any time seize authority in Christ and begin to reign in life!

However, there are those who hold back because they have developed a kind of slave mentality. They have become incapable of forming a mental image of themselves living victoriously. The idea seems to them to be preposterous. Over many years they have developed a complex of inferiority. Their chains have become so familiar they cannot imagine life without them.

They have also persuaded themselves that it is somehow more pious to be abject than to abound, to be miserable than to be merry, to be downtrodden than to be overcoming.

There may also be a pernicious desire within them to offer a personal atonement for sins by the daily sufferings they endure, a kind of stubborn and rebellious refusal to accept forgiveness and victory as free gifts from God.

There is truly a pride hidden in each one of us that presses us to add some personal merit to the merits of Christ. We are all subject to the subtle sin of trying to earn some of our throne rights, instead of humbly accepting them by faith. But God will have none of it. It will be by grace through faith, or it will not be at all!

The remedy for these ills is thorough repentance, renunciation of all dependence on personal worth, and a resolve to possess by faith alone all that God has made freely available in Christ.

CONFESSION

There is no escape from this spiritual law: you will possess it when you confess it! To see it, you must first say it!

Say you are defeated by your enemy, and your slavery will deepen. Say you are reigning with Christ, and your authority will increase. What you say, you will get.

So if you want to reign in life, start talking like a person who is already reigning in life. If you want to be a king, start thinking and speaking like one who is already a king!

Why? Because the authority God has given us in Christ can be exercised only in one way: through the spoken word. It cannot be expressed in any other way, for it is not physical or mechanical, but spiritual. We must exercise divine authority the same way God does, by speaking. His word on your voice, when spoken with faith, has the same authority as when he speaks.

So you will reign in life when you say you are. Your enemy will be defeated when you say he is. Your personal experience of the triumph of Christ can go no further than your confession of that triumph.

If your confession is hesitant, doubtful, ever-changing, so will be your experience of reigning in life. But a bold and persistent confession will irresistibly attract to you all of the resources of heaven's throne, enabling you to joyfully complete all that lies in God's purpose for your life.

Notice the word "*persistent*". The enemy may well decline to yield before one single word of command. He may test the durability of your faith. He may wonder if you really mean it. But if you maintain your command, never wavering from a confident assertion of your rights in Christ, then your triumph will be inevitable. The enemy will be constrained to yield. Your seat upon the throne will become ever more secure.

CHRIST

The walk of faith begins and ends with Christ. "You have everything when you have Christ, and you are filled with God through your union with Christ. He is the highest Ruler, with authority over every other power" (Col 2:10, Taylor).

So then, do not depend upon yourself, nor boast any way in yourself. But let your confidence be in Jesus, not looking to yourself, but

> *"looking to Jesus the pioneer and perfecter of our faith, who for the joy that was set before him endured the cross, despising the shame, and is now seated at the right hand of the throne of God" (He 12:2).*

We who believe in him, are seated with him, on that same throne, reigning in life!

HIDDEN WITH CHRIST IN GOD

See Col 3:1-11.

Paul mentions a batch of sins on account of which, he says, "*the wrath of God is coming.*" He lists them as: immorality, impurity, passion, evil desire, covetousness, anger, wrath, malice, slander, foul talk, deceit, and the like.

Those things are a terror to many Christians, who seem to be quite unable to shake themselves loose from their grip. Despite many tears of repentance the flesh appears to maintain its control over their lives.

Then there are other children of God for whom conversion to Christ, far from ridding them of sin, seems to have made them more abundantly sinful. Sin looms larger in their lives now than it did before they met Christ. In the light of his holy presence they have become aware of a mess of sin which previously they had not dreamed existed. Like a scurrying group of disgusting slugs and insects exposed when you lift up a rock, so sin has been disturbed and revealed within them.

Such people, then, thinking that sin is still rife in their flesh, and knowing that sin must arouse divine anger, feel that they have failed as Christians, and they tremble at the prospect of losing the grace of God.

Many years ago I was in a similar strait. I had struggled with the flesh unavailingly until finally, in spiritual anguish, I bowed myself in prayer and cried out to God for a solution to this awful dilemma. While I was still praying I began to read the third chapter of Colossians, and I was startled to realise (for the first time) that Paul was not addressing the ungodly, but the godly, a group of people whom he said were "*the holy people of God, risen with Christ, the recipients of glory*" - yet he also accused them of some quite ghastly sins!

They were "*dead with Christ*", yet anger, malice, and slander were not uncommon among them. They were "*raised with Christ*", yet Paul could charge them with foul talk and deceit. Their lives were "*hidden with Christ in God*", yet they were still guilty of immorality, evil desire, and covetousness. They were among those who would "*appear with Christ in glory,*" yet passion and impurity could still rule them.

How is it possible for Paul, in the same breath, to accuse people of such sins and yet declare that they are complete in Christ? What solution does he offer for the problem of sin?

A GREAT AFFIRMATION (VS. 1-3)

There are two sides to the problem of sin: the first is our need for pardon; the second is our need for victory. Pardon is, of course, the prerequisite for victory; but pardon is not a guarantee of victory, for there are many who obtain divine forgiveness for their sin, yet do not manage to overcome it. That is because pardon is based on acknowledgment, while victory is based on affirmation.

We obtain pardon from God simply by acknowledging that we have sinned, and by asking him to forgive us: "If we say we have no sin, we deceive ourselves, and the truth is not in us. If we confess our sins, he is faithful and just, and will forgive our sins and cleanse us from all unrighteousness ... the blood of Jesus his Son cleanses us from all sin" (1 Jn 1:7-9).

There can be no victory over sin until we have first obtained divine pardon. But once sin has been confessed, and assurance of forgiveness received, then, in order to overcome sin, a second process must begin, and that is the process of affirmation.

By "*affirmation*" I mean a refusal to allow any sin to deter you from boldly declaring what you are in Christ. You will become no more than you declare yourself to be in Christ. Attention should be focussed on sin only during the few moments in which you repent of it, confess it to God, and seek his pardon. But once that is done, your eyes should then be turned away from yourself as a sinner and fastened onto the glorious image of yourself as a new creation in Christ.

Conquest is gained, not by fighting sin, but by affirming Christ. The reason is obvious: it is not part of God's program that we should renew the war which Christ has already waged and won. He fought and destroyed sin at Calvary. Now our only hope of victory is to enter by faith into his triumph. We have no victory of our own, nor any possibility, by our own struggles, of obtaining one.

So once you have secured pardon for sin by trusting in the blood of Jesus, you should, without further recrimination, guilt, or delay, resume the confident affirmation that -

"I HAVE DIED WITH CHRIST" (VS. 3)

Every believer is fully united with Christ in his death at Calvary, and as a result has passed beyond the reach of all that lies in his previous life. This is a moment by moment fact. Each time I affirm that I am dead with Christ, at that moment I die once again to all of my former life.

An illustration: no matter what crimes a citizen may have committed against the state, the moment he dies he passes beyond the reach of the law. No charges can be raised against him, no penalty can be exacted from him, no enemy can pursue him, no harm can be done to him. He is dead. He has entered a different realm. Nothing that existed in his former world can touch him ever again.

That is the gist of Paul's argument in Ro 7:4-6 ...

> *"Likewise, my brethren, you have died to the law through the body of Christ, so that you may belong to another, to him who has been raised from the dead in order that we may bear fruit for God ... But now we are discharged from the law, dead to that which held us captive, so that we serve not under the old written code but in the new life of the Spirit."*

Paul is talking about a faith-reckoning that enables me to look upon the dead body of Jesus and identify it as my own. I take the stance of a man who is on the other side of death. I have died in Christ, and now I find myself standing away from my dead body, looking on it, and realising that it creates an unpassable barrier between me and the world I have left. I cannot reach back to that world. It cannot reach over to me. My old existence and my new existence are separated irrevocably the moment I reckon myself dead in Christ.

Now it is evident that two things are true of a dead man: the law cannot punish him for any crimes he may have committed; he cannot commit any further crimes.

Our case is the same. Being dead with Christ we escape the penalty of God's broken law (which would have been death, without Christ); and, if we truly know that we are "*dead*", then we gain a basis on which to escape all of our former bondage to the flesh. If you are dead, then you must also be dead to sin.

That is why Paul writes ...

> *"How can we who have died to sin in Christ still live in it? Do you not know that all of us who have been baptised into Christ Jesus were baptised into his death? Yes, we were truly buried with him by baptism into death, and we are therefore united with him in his death. Now you should know that your old self was crucified with him so that your sinful body might be destroyed, and that you might no longer be enslaved by sin. For when a man dies he is freed from sin. So if you have died with Christ, then you must also reckon yourself to be dead to sin" (paraphrased from Ro 6:2-11).*

So then, understanding that you are dead with Christ should lead you to reckon that you are also dead to sin. You should see that the chains that bound you to your sin have been broken by death. You should joyfully affirm that your old habits, your old nature, your old imprisonment, have all been terminated at Christ's grave. They were buried with the body of Jesus.

However, no true servant of God can be content to remain only in a state of passive escape from death, or from guilt and sin. We fervently desire also to be active servants of righteousness. So

Paul, having said "*you have died with Christ*" (Col 3:3), insists also that you must declare ...

"I HAVE BEEN RAISED WITH CHRIST" (VS. 1)

Those who participate in the death of Christ must inevitably share in his resurrection. We cannot die with him without also being raised with him. If his death leads to the eradication of sin, then his resurrection leads to the creation of righteousness -

> *"We were buried with him by baptism into death, so that as Christ was raised from the dead by the glory of the Father, we too might walk in newness of life. For if we have been united with him in a death like his, we shall certainly be united with him in a resurrection like his ... The death he died he died to sin, once for all, but the life he lives he lives to God. So you also must consider yourselves dead to sin and alive to God in Christ Jesus ... Yield yourselves therefore to God as men who have been brought from death to life" (Ro 6:4-13).*

How emphatic he is! You are to declare yourself risen with Christ no matter what your actual circumstances, or your outward state, may be. In your flesh, in your daily practice, many sins may exist, such as those of which he accused the Colossians (vs. 5-9); but this does not deter Paul for a moment from affirming that you are still quite dead with Christ and surely risen with him.

Mark it again, the "*death*" and "*resurrection*" of the Colossians did not depend upon their earthly condition, but upon the completed work of Christ. Christ has already once died, never to die again, and he is truly risen from the dead. Just as truly, all who believe in him, whether or not they have overcome sin, are dead with him, and raised with him into the heavenlies. We are now "*where Christ is, seated at the right hand of God*" (vs. 1).

Whether you are defeated or victorious, living in sin or righteousness, full of faith or despair, whatever your state may be, if you believe in Jesus then scripture demands that you declare yourself dead with Christ, risen with Christ, and seated with him on the throne of authority at God's right hand!

You are not required to gain mastery over sin before you dare to assert that you are enthroned with Christ. If you decide to wait until your righteousness is an earthly fact before you begin affirming it as heavenly reality, you will still be waiting when you die! But if you decide to begin now to accept your position on the throne with Christ, then it will not be long before the heavenly reality becomes an earthly fact. Victory begins with an affirmation that you are already victorious!

"MY LIFE IS HID WITH CHRIST IN GOD" (VS. 3)

Paul's intention, when he wrote to the Colossians, was naturally to turn them away from sin they were committing. He shuddered when he learned that they were still practising the same wickedness they had committed before they knew Christ. He felt sick in his spirit at the bad report that had reached him. He grieved that they were still ruled by their old natures. They were Christians, yet they were guilty of lying, immorality, passion, slander, foul talk, and other rottenness.

Such things were unthinkable. He knew that kind of behaviour, if it was maintained, would erode their faith in Christ and entice them away from the church and back into the godless world from which they had been rescued. He knew they were imperilling their salvation and running the risk of falling again under the wrath of God. He yearned to see them displaying the beautiful character of Christ, full of "*compassion, kindness, lowliness, meekness, patience,*" and the like (vs. 12-14). He wanted them to be utterly rid of sin and to be filled with righteousness.

But how would he achieve that transformation? By telling them they were godless reprobates? By damning them as a disgrace to the name of Christ? By threatening them with awful penalties? By castigating them as miserable pagans? That is what many modern preachers do when they are confronted with the problem of sin in Christian people.

But Paul had a better solution. He kept on calling these erring saints "*God's chosen ones, holy and beloved*" (vs. 12), and before he breathed a word about their sin he wrote many stunning paragraphs about the marvel of what Christ had done for them, and about the glory of their position in Christ (1:1-3:4).

Paul's tactic was not to accuse them of being disgraceful sinners, and then to demand that they start living righteously; rather, he began by confirming that they were true Christians, splendidly enthroned, and only then did he insist that they should express in daily life what they already were in Christ.

He did not demand that they become righteous before he would pronounce them righteous. Rather, he showed them that God had already made them his holy saints in Christ. He first offered them perfect security ("*your life is hid with Christ in God*"), and only then, from that safe base, did he rebuke them and urge them to build a life worthy of Jesus.

Unhappily, many preachers nowadays destroy the security of the people of God by placing them under terrible condemnation. Endlessly they accuse God's children of fault and failure. Instead of identifying the people as the holy, beloved saints of God, these preachers name them as outcasts, and strip them of their hope of salvation. The people are required to begin behaving like saints before their pastors will allow them to be called saints.

But scripture shows that you cannot obtain salvation by working your own righteousness; rather, you can work righteousness only after you have first obtained salvation. It is God's free gift to you in Christ. And once the Christian accepts this God-given status it offers him a place of safety from which he can then go on to build a life that reflects the nature of Jesus.

It is impossible to perform the righteousness of Christ from a position of deep personal revulsion. You may justly loathe your old nature and what it does; but you must love the new nature God has imputed to you in Christ. Endless self-accusation, a heavy burden of guilt, a continual sense of condemnation - those attitudes often have an appearance of piety, but they provide no foundation on which to build a life of triumphant righteousness. On the contrary, they are quicksands that will suck the burdened soul into a morass of deeper sin, a complex of deeper guilt.

God has given you and me only one foundation upon which to build personal victory, and that is the position we have in the heavenlies in Christ. And that position is freely given to us, by grace alone, without the addition of any personal merit. If you believe in Jesus, if you have died with him and have been raised with him, if you are seated with him at God's right hand, then it is true of you, as of every believer: "*your life is hid with Christ in God.*"

In that hiding place you are safe, beyond the reach of sin, beyond the reach of guilt, beyond the reach of Satan. From that place you can sally forth without fear to throw down the fortress of the flesh and to raise a new edifice of godly living. With the security of that place as a foundation, you can work steadily to bring your life into conformity with the character of Christ.

But that conformity is gained, not by constant bitter and despairing struggles against sin, but rather by joy-filled affirmations of what God has already made you to be in Christ, and of what he has already given you in the heavenlies.

"I WILL APPEAR WITH CHRIST" (VS. 4)

I am going to risk tedious repetition (because the natural man is so tardy in faith) by saying that Paul was not writing about himself, nor about a group of admirable saints. He was writing to a huddle of sadly defeated Christians. They were falling far, far short of the standards God expects his people to maintain. There was very little evidence of holiness in the life-style of those Colossians.

In many circles today such people would be thrown out of the church, and their claim to be Christians would be rejected as an awful pretence. Yet Paul placed them on the throne with Christ. As far as a position in the heavenlies was concerned, he made no distinction between their enthronement and his. Together with him, and with all who believe, they were (he said) raised with Christ into the heavenlies and safely hidden in God.

Each Christian is faced with a choice here: to believe sense evidence, or the testimony of God. Will you or will you not believe what God says about you? Your senses may tell you that you are a sinner; but God says you are his righteousness in Christ. Your senses may say that you are defeated; but God says you are triumphant in Christ. Your senses may cry that you are a slave; but God insists you are enthroned with Christ.

What is your choice? Will you believe the witness of the flesh, or of scripture? Which knowledge will govern your confession: sense knowledge, or revelation knowledge? You alone can make that choice.

To encourage us to choose what God says, Paul reminds us about an event that every Christian knows will happen one day: "*When Christ who is our life appears, then you also will appear with him in glory*" (vs. 4). What relevance does this have to a defeated Christian? Three things:

(a) No true believer doubts that one day Christ will return, and when he comes it will be with immense power and surpassing glory. If we believe this, then we also know that all who belong to his church will appear with him on that day, and that his glory will then be theirs (Mt 13:43; Ph 3:20,21; 1 Jn 3:2). If this is our destiny, then we should begin now to live like glorious children of God! Having such a hope, how can any Christian remain bowed by sin, depressed by doubt, burdened with guilt, crippled by a slave-mentality?

That is why John, having spoken of the radiant beauty that will transfigure the church when Jesus comes, cannot help but add:

> *"Everyone who thus hopes in Christ, purifies himself as he is pure" (vs. 3).*

And Peter makes a similar comment:

> *"(since these things are so) what sort of persons ought you to be in lives of holiness and godliness, waiting for and earnestly desiring the coming of the day of God ... Therefore beloved, since you wait for these, be zealous to be found by him without spot or blemish, and at peace" (2 Pe 3:11-14).*

(b) But more importantly (and this is what Paul is really stressing in our text), the glory that will appear in the saints in that future day will be no more than an outward manifestation of the glory they possess right now!

In other words, the source of that future glory is already in you, and if it is not in you now, neither will it be in you then

> *"Christ is in you, the hope of glory" (Col 1:27).*

> *"Those whom he has justified, he has also glorified" (Ro 8:30).*

> *"The creation waits with eager longing for the revealing of (the glory of) the sons of God" (vs. 19).*

The glory that is in you right now is veiled behind your flesh, as it was in Jesus during the years of his incarnation. But if that veil could be removed (as it was from Christ on one occasion), then you would shine like the sun, and the dazzling wonder of your beauty would be like that which the disciples saw in the transfigured Christ (see Mt 17:1-2; Mk 9:2-3; Lu 9:28-29; Rev 1:12-16).

That glory cannot for the present be seen by the natural eye, but it can be discerned by faith. You can gain an inner vision of it, and if you do so, you will inevitably begin to express it in life.

(c) Paul is saying that when Christ appears in his glory, then your true state will also appear. It will be no more true on that day than it is today. It will merely become apparent to the eyes of all.

Do you believe what scripture says about the glory Christ will have on that day? Are you willing to say joyfully that when Jesus comes he will appear in dazzling glory? Then you should be just as willing to believe that the same glory of Christ is in you now, and to say just as joyfully that you are a child of that glory.

As much as you believe the word of God concerning Christ, so you should believe the same word concerning yourself.

Of what use is it to believe that Christ will appear in glory, unless you believe that you also will appear in glory with him? Of what use to look forward happily to the manifestation of your true state on that day, unless you allow that glad anticipation to lead you to this confident affirmation today: "*I am now what I will be then, a glorified son of God, and in that glory I shall live to the praise of the Christ who is in me!*"

Do not wait until you have overcome all sin before commencing that affirmation. It is true right now, and you should confess it right now. Ask yourself the question: "*If Christ came at this moment, would I at once cast aside my mortal flesh, blazon forth in the splendour of the new creation, and leap to meet him in the air, gloriously transfigured into his likeness?*"

If you can give an affirmative answer to that question, then you are simply saying, despite any outward defeat you may be experiencing, that all of the glory of the coming resurrection is in you now. Your acknowledgment of this fact, and your affirmation of it, will release the power of it into your daily walk.

A GREAT ADMONITION

Paul lays down three rules by which we can grasp the marvellous revelation of what God has wrought for us in Christ, and then make it work for us in life -

(1) "SEEK THE THINGS THAT ARE ABOVE" (VS. 1)

That is an admonition to fix your attention on the heavenlies, "*where Christ is, seated at the right hand of God.*" By prayer, by meditating in God's word, fill your eyes with the vision of Christ enthroned, and enrich your understanding of your position with him on the same throne.

Seek those things! Earnestly inquire after those heavenly realities! Pray through, so that your faith will be vibrant with the revelation of them, singing in the joy of a victory accomplished. Determine to understand them, not just theoretically, but practically. Look at Jesus, not at yourself! The more engrossed your faith becomes with Jesus, the more your life will reflect his beauty and authority.

(2) "SET YOUR MINDS ON THINGS THAT ARE ABOVE" (VS. 2)

That is an admonition to wean yourself away from love of "*things that are on the earth*", and to direct your deepest affection toward Christ in the heavenlies. To have a clear vision of Christ is to love him. But love, to survive and to be fulfilled, must become consummated through an exclusive union. The soul must wed itself to Christ, resolving to be his alone (cp. Ep 5:25-27; 2 Co 11:2). There can be no lasting victory without a total surrender to him.

(3)"PUT TO DEATH ... PUT AWAY ... PUT OFF ... PUT ON"

That is an admonition to act in faith so that your enthronement with Christ in the heavenlies may be expressed through a life of victory on earth. There are two aspects to this faith: the past, and the present - both of them expressed by the verbs "*put off*" and "*put on*".

The past aspect of faith refers to our union through baptism with Christ's burial and resurrection (Col 2:12; 3:1). If you have been so united with him, then you have already -

> *"put off the old nature" and*
>
> *"put on the new nature" (vs. 9-10).*

Since scripture affirms those two things concerning you, you should affirm them concerning yourself. They are simply true. Through baptism God has already acted in your life to put to death your old sinful nature and to create in you a new nature made in his image. That is not something you have to do; it is already done. Paul is emphatic: "*You have put off the old nature ... and you have put on the new nature.*"

As a baptised believer in Christ you are simply asked to believe what God did for you when you were baptised. You may not have felt this transformation taking place; there may not even be any sign as yet in your life that it did take place; but if you are truly a baptised Christian, then you can be assured that this work is done. The scripture does not lie. By virtue of your faith- union with the burial of Christ, through baptism, your old nature has been destroyed; and by virtue of your faith-union with the resurrection of Christ, through baptism, the new nature has been planted within you.

The truth of those statements depends on no work of your own, saving the fact that you believe in Christ and that you have been baptised.[7] If you have faith in the working of God through baptism (Col 2:12), then you can confidently assert: "*My old nature has*

---

[7] I am not expressing any opinion here as to which of the various modes of baptism practised by the churches is the most valid. If you truly believe in Christ as your Lord and Saviour, and have been sincerely baptised according to the mode of your church, then what I have written above is applicable to you.

been buried with Christ, along with all its practices; and now I have received a new nature as God's gift to me in Christ." There is no room for doubt: you have put off the old; you have put on the new.

Your confidence in what God has done in the past should now become the basis for your faith activity in the present. If it is true that you have put off the old nature and put on the new, then you can also now act in faith to put off the works of the old nature, and to put on the works of the new.

So Paul writes:

> *"Put away anger, wrath, malice ... put on compassion, kindness, love" (vs. 8,12,14).*

Your faith in the working of God in baptism is deprived of its value unless you make it the basis on which you, still by faith, cast aside all that belongs to the old nature and set yourself to live by the pattern of your new nature.

Paul uses two more verbs that show this is a continuing work of faith: "*put to death*" and "*being renewed*". He says: "*Put to death therefore what is earthly in you*" (vs. 5). Here is a decision faith makes continually to reckon the old nature and all of its works as dead. It is faith nullifying the power of the old nature and destroying its works by an act of will.

Whenever some "*earthly*" work tries to resurrect itself out of the burial ground of baptism, faith rises against it to declare it dead, to release against it the working of God, and to lay it again in the grave. The godly Christian chooses not to sin; but he wages war against sin, not by personal struggle, not with carnal weapons, but by a faith reckoning and faith confession in Christ, which simply puts sin to death. In this way he puts off both the old nature and its works.

This warfare of faith is continual, and continuing victory depends upon the believer maintaining his vision of "*the things that are above, where Christ is, seated at the right hand of God.*" Unless he has a clear understanding of his identity as a son of God enthroned with Christ in the heavenlies; unless he knows that his life is securely "*hidden with Christ in God*"; unless he maintains his resolve to behave according to the position God has given him in Christ, he will lose confidence in his spiritual authority, his faith confession will waver, and sin will again seize dominion over him.

Your righteousness in Christ, and your glorious position with him at God's right hand, can never be any more real on earth than your apprehension of them by faith.

But Paul promises that knowledge of these things, and an unshakeable faith-affirmation of them, will cause the new nature God has given you to gain increasing ascendancy in your life: "*You have put on the new nature which is being renewed in knowledge after the image of its creator*" (vs. 10). Notice the words "*in knowledge*". As your prayerful study of the word of God opens your understanding, as you come to increasing revelation of the truth of your position in Christ, as you pronounce ever more boldly the death of the old nature, so the new nature will be daily renewed within you, and your life will conform ever more closely to the image of Christ.

CHAPTER FIVE:

ANSWERED PRAYER

"Prayer," said the man, "is bunk! Leave that kind of gobbledygook to old ladies, kids, and finks who are frightened of their own shadow. Prayer I can do without!"

I raised an eyebrow. It was rather strong language. But after talking with him for a while I decided I would have to agree with him - that is, if I held the same notion of prayer as he did. He thought of prayer as nothing more than a religious prop, a sop to ignorant superstition, a last desperate resort when all else had failed. And if that is really all there is to prayer, then we can well do without it!

Needless to say, that man, because he rejected prayer, also rejected the whole Christian religion. He saw clearly what even many Christians fail to see: Christianity stands or falls on its claim of answered prayer.

All religions have practised some form of prayer, but no other faith has ever dared to make the breathtaking claims of answered prayer that the Bible makes.

"*Answered prayer!*" That claim stunned the ancient world. It was one thing about Christianity that was truly unique. Never before had the world seen so many ordinary people so vitally in touch with God and so commonly enjoying miracle after miracle of divine provision. This daily demonstration of the reality of answered prayer drew people by their thousands to worship the living God. The word of the psalmist was fulfilled -

> *"O Thou that hearest prayer, to thee shall all flesh come!" (65:2).*

If our God does not hear and answer prayer, then he has no more relevance than the weird gods of the ancient world, whom the psalmist scorned -

"Their idols ... are silver and gold ... they have mouths, but they speak not; they have eyes but they see not; they have ears, but they hear not. Those that make them are like them!" (135:15-18).

Once again I say, our faith stands or falls on the reality of answered prayer. If God answers prayer, let him be worshipped; if not, let him be rejected. If our God answers prayer, then we can boldly invite "all flesh" to come to him; if not, then men are wise to scorn us and our religion.

So there is hardly anything more important to the church than learning how to pray and receive an answer from heaven. If we want the world to listen to us we have to show that prayer is not merely a religious exercise, a kind of pious escapism, or spiritual narcotic, but that it is the most real thing in the whole world. We must show that prayer, because God does answer it, is the very breath of life, the one thing a person can't do without!

Now this leads me to ask: what kind of prayer does God hear and answer?

FOUR KEYS TO ANSWERED PRAYER

PRAYER THAT IS BASED ON THE AUTHORITY OF SCRIPTURE

There are two ways to look at scripture: one is to see it as the story of man's search for God; the other is to see it as the story of God's search for man.

The first sees the Bible as an expression of man's mind toward God. The second sees it as an expression of God's mind toward man. The first thinks that the Bible is merely a human book, containing many errors; the second finds in the Bible God's revelation of himself to man, a divine authority, a sure guide to faith.

The first view stifles prayer, while the second strengthens it. Why? Simply because prayer is essentially an encounter with God. But where and how can a person meet God? The answer: in his word. Here, in the scriptures, God has revealed himself. Here we can meet him face to face. In fact, all human encounter with God has to begin with his word; and all continuing encounter with him stems from that initial meeting (see Ro 10:14-17).

Hence it follows that only those who have a high view of scripture as the word of God, and who immerse themselves daily in his word, can hope to have an effective and continual experience of answered prayer. The kind of faith that is essential to successful prayer can be nourished and set aflame only by scripture. Prayer divorced from the Bible is either an act of foolish presumption or of religious formality. In either case it will be ignored by God.

PRAYER THAT YOU HAVE A RIGHT TO PRAY

I once read a story about a crusty old preacher. He was in charge of a prayer meeting at which a pious lady decided to intercede for all the missionaries around the world. She began her global tour in England, then jumped across the channel and worked her way through France, Scandinavia and Germany, continued eastward to Russia, and began to work her way toward China and Southeast Asia.

By this time the preacher was getting restless, and when it became obvious that the prayer would not end until the lady had girdled the whole earth with her pleas, he burst out, "*Friends, while our sister is completing her journey, we'll sing a hymn*" - and he swung into song, pulling the rather startled (but relieved) congregation with him!

Was he wrong?

Of course not. The prayer was meaningless, because it was not based on personal involvement. Let me illustrate what I mean.

Suppose you went to a court of law and demanded the right to address the judge on behalf of an accused person. The judge would at once ask on what grounds you demanded that right. Are you a relation of the accused? A friend? His employer? His pastor? But suppose you reply that you have no personal knowledge of the accused, nor of his circumstances, you only feel sorry for him. You will be thrown out of the court!

To be taken seriously on any matter at all you must first earn the right to speak. But that right can come only by learning, experience, relationship - or in some other way that has created in you a deep personal involvement with that matter.

So it is with prayer. If you speak to God about matters on which you have no right to speak, because you have no personal involvement in them, you will not be taken seriously.

That is the principle behind such statements as:

> *"(They) sought God with their whole desire, and he was found by them ... Thou hast given him his heart's desire, and hast not withheld the request of his lips ... The kingdom of heaven suffers violence, and men of violence take it by force ... Strive (struggle earnestly) to enter ... The fervent prayer of a righteous man has great power in its effects" (2 Ch 15:15; Ps 21:2; Mt 11:12; Lu 13:24; Ro 15:30; Ja 5:16).*

So, the kind of prayer that has power with God has in it these elements: personal involvement that leads to deep desire; total commitment to obtaining an answer; fervency, and even a touch of violence.

PRAYER THAT HAS IN IT A FAITH VISION

Michelangelo was walking through a quarry with a friend when suddenly he stopped and stood gazing at a rough slab of marble.

After a few moments he asked, "*What do you see in that block?*" His perplexed friend stared for a while, then shrugged, "*Nothing, except a lump of stone.*" But the sculptor replied, "*I see an angel!*" He arranged for the marble to be shipped to his studio, and then set to work with hammer and chisel. In time a magnificent angel appeared to the wonder of the world.

With his inner vision Michelangelo saw what other men could not see. He saw what could actually be brought into existence out of the formless rock, and he was able to produce it.

Prayer operates on the same principle.

You are unlikely to receive any answer to your prayer unless you can actually "*see*" what you desire coming into existence. If you are not able to visualise the answer to your prayer, and thus know that its realisation is a genuine possibility, you will probably pray in vain.

Be honest with yourself. You are asking God for a miracle. Do you really think it is likely that your prayer will be answered; or, when you think about it, does it seem quite unlikely?

Do you react to the challenge of prayer with a forceful, "*Yes! Of course it can be done; there's no doubt about it. I can see it as clearly as though it has already happened!*" Or are you constrained to chuckle and ruefully to admit that you can't really visualise your miracle happening?

When you try to visualise the answer to your prayer you will always laugh - either with derision or with delight. Sarah heard God promise a son to her and her husband in their old age, and she laughed, in derision. God rebuked her (Ge 18:9-15). Abraham also heard God, and he too laughed, but in delight. His faith was counted to him for righteousness (Ge 17:15-17; 15:4-6).

Sarah looked into the future, and she simply could not see her desire being fulfilled.

Abraham also looked, and saw, and thanked God for the answer. We are urged to follow his example of faith (Ro 4:18-25).

It is worth asking: what is the sound of your laugh when you are offered a miracle?

PRAYER THAT IS CONTENT WITH GOD ALONE.

"Take delight in the Lord, and he will give you the desires of your heart" (Ps. 37:4).

Many people fail in their prayers because their motives are essentially earth-bound; their desires are wholly materialistic; hence they cannot possibly touch the spiritual realm where God dwells. The true end of all prayer must be the discovery of God himself.

Whatever you seek in prayer you should seek, not for its own sake alone, but for the greater understanding of God you can gain from the answer to your prayer. Your highest desire must be to glorify God, not to gratify yourself.

Why should you ask for healing? Because you want to delight yourself in God as the Great Physician! Why should you ask for deliverance from sin? Because you want to delight yourself in God as the Great Saviour! Why should you ask for your financial need to be met? Because you want to delight yourself in God as the Great Provider!

Why should you ask for comfort and fellowship? Because you want to delight yourself in God as the Great Father! And so on ..

James wrote: "You do not have because you do not ask. You ask, and do not receive, because you ask wrongly" (4:2-3). But if you ask, and ask properly, with delight in the Lord himself, then you will certainly receive. His promise will then be true for you: "Ask and you will receive, that your joy may be full" (Jn 16:24).

FOUR STEPS TO A MIRACLE

A young man once came to me and said, "Pastor, tell me in three easy steps how to get a miracle!"

I said, "I can't do it in three steps; but I'll try four."

And I told him.

He answered me with astonishment, "Is that all there is to it?"

There are, of course, many more than four things to say about how to offer a prayer of faith. But the four steps which follow are sufficient to bring anyone a miracle of answered prayer.

KNOW WHAT GOD WANTS

Many years ago the Tasmanian Government appointed a Parliamentary Select Committee to investigate the wisdom of building a casino in Launceston (where I was then living). Submissions for and against the casino proposal were invited from the general public, and I resolved to prepare a case against it. The appointed day arrived for me to appear before the committee and to present my case.

Unhappily, I had been unable to find out just what was expected of me - should I argue the case informally? Should I just read aloud my submission? Would the members read it and ask me questions?

So I approached the committee with much uncertainty, and felt far from confident when the interview began. Some fifteen minutes later it was all over, and I was outside again, not very happy with my performance.

What was the problem?

Simply that I did not know what was expected of me, nor how much in the way of argument the committee was prepared to accept. So my speech was hesitant and restrained. But now that I have faced a parliamentary committee, and know what is permissible and required from those who appear before it, I will approach my encounter with a very different frame of mind!

What is the lesson here?

Simply that freedom and boldness in speech arise from knowing how much is expected of you, and how much your hearer is prepared to accept from you. Without this, your petition will be unsure, tinged with hesitancy, lacking in authority.

The Greeks had a word for this: "*parrhesia*". It has the same sense that we mean when we talk about the democratic privilege of "*freedom of speech*" - that is, being able to speak boldly, without fear of tyranny. It is freedom to stand before the mightiest in the land and to speak your convictions without reserve, and without fear of arbitrary punishment.

John uses "parrhesia" when he writes, "This is the confidence we have in him, that if we ask anything according to his will he hears us" (1 Jn 5:14).

John is saying that boldness of speech before God, freedom in prayer, spiritual authority, can be ours only when we know that we are asking for something God wants us to have.

So the first vital step in answered prayer is this: find out what God wants. Without that you cannot be sure that God is listening to you when you pray. Before you can gain victory over the habit that binds you, or the supply of some material need, or the healing of your physical disease, or whatever it is you are asking God to do for you, you must first be sure that you are praying "*according to his will*".

Now that phrase, "*according to his will,*" sounds dully negative to many people. As soon as they hear it they get a mental image of prayer imprisoned, confined, restricted. The thought is enough to deter them altogether from praying. They feel that prayer is useless, because they are convinced that the will of God is so narrow their request will certainly be denied.

How wrong they are! Prayer will be limited, not by praying according to the will of God, but by failing to pray according to his will! The promise of God is so large, it encompasses so many good things, that if you should resolve to have all that lies in his will for your life, you would be blessed beyond your wildest expectations!

We are poor, not because we do submit to the will of God, but because we do not submit to it. Our prayers are vacuous, not because we ask for more than God desires to give, but because we hardly even begin to ask for what he has promised!

He says to you in scripture,

> *"Beloved, I wish above all things that you may prosper and be in health, even as your soul prospers more abundantly ... Ask and you shall receive, that your joy may be full ... I am able to provide you with every blessing in abundance, so that you may always have enough of everything and may provide in abundance for every good work ... Delight yourself in me, and I will give you the desires of your heart!"*

Our problem is that we are often content to have less than God's best - content to be poor when he wants to give abundantly, to be defeated when he wants to confer victory, to be sick when he wants to bring healing, to be dismal when he wants to create happiness.

Because we do not take the trouble to discover the purpose of God, because we have only vague ideas about what his will for us might be, our lives are often marked by paucity rather than plenty, and by poverty rather than prosperity.

The greatest release in prayer that you could experience would spring out of a firm and enthusiastic resolution to possess all of the marvellous blessings that are part of God's will for you. You can be quite sure of this: if you take time to discover what God really wants to do for you, you will discover a storehouse of good things so vast it will overwhelm you with delight. It is still true of most people that their "eyes have not seen, nor have their ears heard, nor has it entered into their hearts, what God has prepared for those who love him." But he is willing to "reveal these things to us by his Spirit." (See 1 Co 2:9-13).

Confidence in prayer arises from knowing the will of God. And the will of God includes more healing, more happiness, more personal fulfilment, more success, more victory, more achievement, more prosperity than you have ever dreamed possible. His desire for you is the same as it was for David:

> *"I anointed you king over Israel, and I delivered you out of the hand of Saul, and I gave you your master's house, and your master's wives into your bosom, and gave you the house of Israel and of Judah; and if this were too little, I would add to you as much more" (2 Sa 12:7-8).*

The Living Bible translates the last clause as: "*If that had not been enough, I would have given you much, much more.*" <u>That</u> is the measure of God's desire for you: he wants to give you much, much more!

But to know only that God wants you to prosper, to have "*much more*", is still an inadequate base for successful prayer. The questions arise, "*much more*" of what? In what areas does he want you to prosper? How does he want you to succeed? What kind of happiness does he want you to have?

Those questions can be answered only by arriving at a more particular understanding of the purpose of God for your own life. His promise of prosperity and of abundant life is differently outworked in each person.

Basically, there are four ways by which you can discover the will of God in your present situation

(1) FROM SCRIPTURE

Here there are promises of God that cover our deepest needs - of pardon, of physical healing, of eternal life, of personal victory, of inner peace and love. Whenever your need is covered by a promise of God there can be no longer any doubt as to what God is willing to do for you. Be bold to claim the promise and to expect a miracle!

(2) FROM PRAYER

Sometimes you are faced with a need for which you can discover no specific promise in scripture. In this case, seek the will of God in prayer; he is well able to speak deep in your heart and to reveal his desire to you - see Is 30:21; Col 3:15; Ja 1:5.

(3) FROM WISE COUNSEL

See Pr 11:14. If several people who are spiritually mature, and competent to offer counsel, agree in the advice they give you, it is probable that their advice will be in harmony with the will of God.

(4) FROM SPIRITUAL GIFTS

Those who worship in a charismatic or pentecostal church can thank God that they have this additional means of discovering his will: the Lord often speaks to people through prophecy, interpretation of tongues, or through one of the other gifts of the Holy Spirit.

When you know what God wants, then you can pray with confidence, sure that he will hear you, and sure that you already have the good thing you are asking for (1 Jn 5:14-15).

WANT WHAT GOD WANTS

You will not make much progress in prayer so long as you are content to have less than God's best. Your deepest desire should be to have all that God has promised. How can you be content not to have the promise of God realised in your life? You should be utterly resolved to have everything God has shown you he wants you to have - whether it is a little thing or a large one.

Many people pray for something because they believe they should pray for it - as a matter of duty, or conscience - not because they really want the thing they are praying for.

They may be asking God to rid them of a certain sin, and by this they salve their guilt; but their prayer is not heard because they are still in love with that sin and are not really willing to let go of it.

I have met people who pray for healing because, having been faced with the healing promise of God, their conscience drives them to ask God to make them well. But though they ask for healing, they don't really want it, for they enjoy the sympathetic care and attention their sickness brings them. So, of course, they are not healed. Neither God nor man can make them well against their own will.

There are some women who are married to harsh and brutal men, and who pray for their husband's conversion because they feel they ought to pray for it; but they pray without any real conviction or desire, because deep inside they gain a kind of masochistic satisfaction from being dominated and ill-treated. Such a woman, even if she sees signs of her husband being converted, will often unconsciously provoke him to anger again and so turn him away from Christ.

There are churches praying for revival that have no chance of seeing their prayer answered, for they are not willing to face the demands upon their time, ambitions, and self-indulgence, that a great outpouring of the Holy Spirit would make. The most costly thing in every way (spiritually, emotionally, physically, financially, socially) that can happen to any church is a powerful revival. Christians sense this, and while they pray for revival, because they feel they must, all the time they are actually willing that their prayer should be ignored.

There are people who pray for personal victory, or for freedom from some enslaving habit, or for a new experience of spiritual authority, or for a new level of success and prosperity; but secretly they hope their prayer will remain unheard. Perhaps they have developed a slave mentality and prefer bondage to freedom? Perhaps they are frightened by the thought of having an abundance of anything (except depression and poverty) because of the responsibilities to God and neighbour that prosperity entails? Perhaps, not being content with the full atonement God offers them in Christ, they have a perverted desire to punish themselves for sin and to build their own righteousness by the things they suffer? Perhaps they are using their defeat to condemn themselves as unworthy to serve God; thus they build an excuse to avoid the front-line of spiritual battle?

So I could go on citing examples of people who pray for something because they know God wants them to have it, but who don't really want it themselves. There is little chance their prayer will be answered!

But of course, we don't really have any option in this matter. We become guilty of the sin of rebellion against the will of God if we refuse to want what God wants.

So a second (and essential) step in answered prayer is this: having discovered what God wants, get to work on yourself until there is distilled within your soul a passionate longing for that thing, a longing that refuses to rest until the will of God is realised in your life.

NOURISH YOUR FAITH

Faith is not merely a mechanical force. It is a living thing. And like any living thing it must be nourished or it will die. Furthermore, for each new need a new faith must be born, nourished, and expanded.

In this, faith is like the manna the Israelites gathered during their wanderings through the desert. That manna was like some modern bread - it has to be gathered in the morning and eaten the same day, for on the next day it is not fit to eat!

> *"Moses said to them, 'Let no man keep any of the manna overnight.' But they did not listen to Moses; some left part of it till the morning, and it bred worms and became foul; and Moses was angry with them" (Ex 16:4ff).*

Because a person has previously gained a miracle of answered prayer he is often inclined to take it for granted that when he prays again he will get the same result. He tries to bring yesterday's faith into today's need. But that old faith is stale, it has been expended, its strength is gone. A new need demands the creating and nourishing of a new faith.

One of the best ways to do that is to

CONSIDER THE POWER OF GOD

Think about the power of God. When did you last wonder about just what power God has, or ask yourself just what he can do, in which direction does his power move, what action does it take, and so on?

Many people think of the power of God only in a vague or abstract sense, or they speak of it only in the terms of some theological doctrine. So they never discover the real strength of God, they never feel his touch. You should learn to believe in the power of God in a real and personal sense, to have an inner awareness, a vital consciousness of it.

Christ had that kind of awareness in mind when he said, "*Nothing is too hard for God,*" and "*With God all things are possible, and nothing shall be impossible!*" When the Lord spoke those words he was not just preaching a nice doctrine, nor uttering some wise sayings about divine omnipotence. Far from it! He was talking from the depths of his personal experience of the Father's power. He was endeavouring to show us that we can have that same experience!

I have shown you earlier that Paul spoke about this vivid personal awareness of the power of God: "*I pray that you may know the immeasurable greatness of his power in us who believe*" (Ep 1:16-20).

The apostle prayed for two things: that you might know the enormous ability of God; and that you might know that all of this divine ability is directed toward you. In other words, when scripture talks about the power of God, it does so, not to provide a debating point for scholars, but to show what God is able to do for you.

Right now, at this point in history, the immense power of God, the power that created the universe and raised Jesus from the dead is dedicated to your deliverance. By faith you can meet that power. To have the touch of God is the greatest thing on earth; it is worth all you possess; but God asks from you only faith - for his power is "*in us who believe*"!

THE EXAMPLE OF ABRAHAM

Abraham is a good example of a man who nourished his faith by contemplating the power of God:

> *"(Having been told that he would be the father of many nations) he did not weaken in faith when he considered his own body, which was as good as dead because he was about a hundred years old, or when he considered the barrenness of Sarah's womb. No distrust made him waver concerning the promise of God, but he grew strong in faith as he gave glory to God, fully convinced that God was able to do what he had promised" (Ro 4:19-21).*

Like Abraham, you can create faith in your heart, and nourish it

- by getting a promise from God that guarantees the supply of your need.

- by becoming fully convinced that God is able to do whatever he has promised.
- by refusing to yield to anything except the promise, no matter how impossible it may seem.
- by giving glory to God for your coming miracle!

RELEASE YOUR FAITH

Like a ferret kept to hunt rabbits, faith, to be effective, must be released.

The ferret will do no good if he is kept locked up in a cage; neither will faith, if it remains imprisoned in your heart. You must turn faith loose before it can do its mighty work.

So look ahead, and set a specific time and place when you will determine to believe and receive the answer to your prayer.

I am always pleased when someone comes to me and says, "*Pastor, next Sunday I am going to ask you to pray with me about (whatever the need may be).*" Such people show that they are making proper preparations for a miracle; and it also gives me an opportunity to ready my own faith for the moment of prayer.

Many of the major miracles that have taken place in my own life have occurred through the use of this principle of releasing faith at a particular point.

On each of those occasions, faced with an important need,

- I set about obtaining a promise from God that guaranteed an answer to that need then I set myself a time and a place, a week or so ahead, when I resolved to release faith in that promise
- and then I applied myself to the enjoyable task of enriching and strengthening my faith in God in respect to that particular promise.
- **And each time the miracle was wrought**.

Not always instantaneously - for sometimes there is a waiting period during which, having claimed the answer from God, one must stand with unwavering confidence until that answer materialises. But come it will, if you trust and do not doubt.

Now there are some objects of prayer, of course, where this process may not be suitable. For example, in the matter of the salvation of a loved one, or of revival in the church, or of discovering God's purpose for your life, and so on, it may be impossible to set a particular point at which you can release your faith.

In such cases you can do no more than persevere in believing prayer until the answer comes, in God's time, and God's way. But in all those other cases, if you will do the four things I have suggested (assuming you are a committed Christian) I am sure you will gain the answer to your prayer. It's true. That's all there is to it!

CHAPTER SIX:

WORDS THAT CREATE MIRACLES

God is ABLE!
He is able to do what you ASK.
He is able to do ALL that you ask.
He is able to do ABOVE all that you ask.
He is able to do above all that you ask or THINK.
He is able to do ABUNDANTLY above all that you ask or think.

- in fact,

"He is able to do ***EXCEEDING*** *abundantly above all that we can ask or even think!" (Ep 3:20).*

With those breath-taking words, Paul gives an arresting statement of the immense ability of God to answer prayer. Our God is able to give us far more than we could ever desire or even dream!

But now we are faced with a peculiar difficulty.

If God is so able, why do so few people experience this wealth of answered prayer? After all, how many of us find God doing even what we ask, let alone "*exceeding abundantly above*" all that we ask?

An answer is found in the relationship between ....

GOD'S ABILITY AND YOUR ABILITY

Our text presents the startling idea that the exercise of God's ability is linked to the exercise of our ability. The measure of answered prayer, said Paul, is "*according to the ability at work within us.*" Here is the entire verse, in a literal translation from Paul's Greek -

"God is able above all measure to do super-abundantly all that we ask or think, according to the ability that is operating in us[8] *"*

Notice the couplet, "*God is able ... we are able,*" linked by the prepositional phrase "*according to.*" In the Greek, that preposition is "*kata*", and in this place it has the sense of one thing conforming to another, or of one thing being in proportion to another. It expresses the limits within which divine ability will ordinarily operate on our behalf. It conveys the sense that God is indeed "*able*", but his working on our behalf cannot exceed the working of certain ability which is in us.

There is no limit, of course, on the power of God itself, which is boundless. But the outworking of that power in your life will usually be in proportion to the use of your own power. His "*working*" conforms to your "*working*". The exercise of his ability depends upon the exercise of your ability.

So the verse could also be rendered, "God is able to do exceeding abundantly above all that we ask or think, in proportion to the ability that is at work within us."

Or again, there are some things only God can do, and there are some things only you can do. When you do what only you can do, God will do what only he can do. Put your ability to work, and you will see a corresponding working of divine ability!

What is this "*ability*" that is at work within us?

---

[8] Paul uses the verb "*dunamai*" ("*God is able*"), and the cognate noun "*dunamis*" ("*the power*"). Dunamai means "*to be able*"; and likewise dunamis, which means "*ability*", along with "*power*" and "*strength*". Some translators choose "*power*" for "*dunamis*" in Ep 3:20, but I think the meaning of the verse is improved by choosing "*ability*". It then reads as I have indicated above: "*(God) is able to do exceeding abundantly above all that we ask or think, according to the ability at work within us.*" Dunamis may indeed carry the sense of supernatural power, of force and strength; but it often prefers the sense of "*ability*" - cp. Mt 25:14; 2 Co 8:3 ("*means*", twice); Re 18:3 ("*wealth*").

No doubt there are many possible responses to that question.

But here I want to suggest just three things, which I know you already have, and which, if rightly used, will bring you to a place where all of God's immense power can act on your behalf

THE POWER TO CHOOSE

The ability to make a truly intelligent choice is unique to man. No animal has this power. True, animals can choose to go here or there, to walk or to run, to kill or to spare - but their choices are mainly instinctive. They are incapable of moral choice, or of choosing to act contrary to their own nature.

But man has been given the supreme prerogative of the highest level of intelligent moral choice. Man possesses a power of choice that does not seem to be possessed in the same degree even by the holy angels. It is part of the divine image that lies in us. Because of it, we can choose to raise ourselves to the highest heaven, or to thrust ourselves into the deepest hell. We can choose to live nobly or ignobly, to be ruled by faith or fear, to create or to destroy, to love or to hate, to war against God or to serve him joyfully.

If you think for a moment, you will realise that all of life is a succession of choices. We are constantly being forced to decide between two courses of action, to determine what attitudes we shall adopt, what character we shall display, what emotion will dominate our lives.

Our ultimate destiny is irrevocably determined by the cumulative effect of the choices we make each day.

Likewise, all of our dealings with God begin with a choice. That is why the great challenge was given to Israel -

> *"I call heaven and earth to witness against you this day, that I have set before you life and death, blessings and curses; therefore <u>choose life</u>, that you and your descendants may live ... <u>Choose</u> this day whom you will serve!" (De 30:19; Js 24:15).*

And just as Moses challenged Israel to make a right choice, so too, in our text, Paul is thrusting a choice upon us. He sets before us the tremendous strength of God. He says "*GOD IS ABLE!*" Then he lays down a challenge to choose: choose to believe that God is able; choose to believe that with overwhelming generosity, with irresistible might, he can and will meet your need; and refuse to accept the possibility that the Lord is unable or unwilling to hear your cry.

To put it simply: you can step towards a miracle, first, by accepting that God is able ; and then by deciding, deep in your heart, that you will resolutely depend on him to do abundantly what you ask.

So long as your choice lies within the scope of his broad promise, it will be done.

THE POWER TO HOLD TO YOUR CHOICE

Making a right choice is important. But it is even more important, once that choice is made, to stick to it.

Many people decide to believe the promise of God, but then, because the answer is delayed, or because opposition rises up against them, they waver, turn aside, and change their minds. To people like that the Bible warns -

> *"Ask in faith, with no doubting, for he who doubts is like a wave of the sea that is driven and tossed by the wind. For that person must not suppose that a double minded man, unstable in all his ways, will receive anything from the Lord" (Ja 1:6-8).*

This fact must be faced: a "*double minded*" person, full of faith one day but full of doubt the next, praying with great boldness today but grumbling against God tomorrow, will receive nothing from God.

By contrast, in the face of delay, of setback, of opposition, the man or woman of faith will stand firm, refusing to be shifted from a joyful expectation that the promise received from God will be abundantly fulfilled.

There is such a thing as "*the trial of faith*". We pray. We believe. Then comes the testing.

During this time of waiting for the answer to appear, do you hold to your choice, or do you become discouraged and reject the promise of God? Yet the trial itself should be a thing of joy to you - for does not scripture say that the proving of your faith is a thing "*more precious than gold*", and that it will "*redound to praise and glory and honour at the revelation of Jesus Christ*"? (1 Pe 1:6-7).

So, thousands of people cheat themselves out of a miracle simply because, having chosen to believe and to pray, they do not stay by that choice until the answer comes.

Job was not like that. He cried out, "*Though he slay me, yet will I trust him!*" And out of his mighty, unshakeable determination, was born the faith that brought to Job a dramatic miracle of healing and untold prosperity and happiness.

The army of Israel resolved to believe God, and to go and conquer the Philistines. But then they saw the vast Philistine host, and their faith vanished like a desert mirage. Terror seized them. They all fled for their very lives. All, that is, except one man, Eleazar. He laughed, stood his ground, drew his sword, and cried, "*I believe God!*" Then he fought until the Philistines lay in heaps all around him, and the Lord "*wrought a great victory that day.*" The rest of the Israelites came back to rob the bodies of the Philistines only when the battle was won. One man, despite overwhelming odds, held to his choice, and a wonderful miracle took place! (2 Sa. 23:8-12).

Exhausted and hungry in the fierce wilderness, the Lord Jesus Christ scorned Satan's temptation, saying, "*Man shall not live by bread alone, but by every word of God.*" He declared that he would perish rather than shift from his resolve to believe and to obey his

Father. So the angels came, and succoured him; the Holy Spirit fell upon him in power; and the devil was driven away.

Here then is an important ingredient in successful prayer: set yourself to believe the promise of God, and then, come what may, hold to that choice.

THE POWER OF A RIGHT CONFESSION

One of the greatest powers we possess is the power of speech. This ability, like the power of choice, is also unique to man. It is part of our likeness to God, for it seems that only God and man have the power to create or to destroy simply by speaking.

The exercise of this power ordinarily determines the measure by which God answers prayer. It is almost always true to say that no man's prayer or faith can rise above the level of his confession. What you say you will get.

If the things you say are contrary to the will of God, if you express doubt about his promise, if you complain about his ways, you may make it impossible for your prayer to be heard.

On the other hand, if you boldly affirm faith in the promise of God, if you declare your decision to believe that promise, if you uphold that choice with an unwavering confidence in the ability of the Lord, then you will open a channel through which all of heaven's supply can flow to meet your need!

No wonder James writes -

> *"We can make a large horse turn around and go wherever we want by means of a small bit in his mouth. And a tiny rudder makes a huge ship turn wherever the pilot wants it to go, even though the wind is strong. So also the tongue is a small thing, but what enormous results it can cause. A great forest can be set on fire by one tiny spark" (Ja 3:3-5).*

There is a vast power of good, and of evil, reserved in your tongue. It is imperative, if you wish to enjoy continual success in prayer, to bring your tongue under discipline, and steadfastly to maintain a bold, positive, confession of faith.

You can talk your way out of, or into, answered prayer!

Here is another significant verse on this matter ....

THE HIGH PRIEST OF OUR CONFESSION

> *"Therefore, holy brethren, who share in a heavenly call, consider Jesus, the apostle and high priest of our confession" (He 3:1).*

In the life of prayer, this passage is one of the most vital in the whole Bible. It tells us that God has chosen Christ to be our Apostle and our High Priest.

As our "*Apostle*", Christ has been given mighty power to act on our behalf, to meet our needs, and to bring us to good news of God's mercy and kindness.

As our "*High Priest*", Christ has been given the right to make a sacrifice on our behalf and to intercede for us before the Father's throne.

We have dire need of those two things. We need someone who can reconcile us to God. And we need someone who can break the chains of sin and sickness, of fear and death, which so sorely bind us.

Christ has that power.

He can loose us from every bondage, and he can restore us to fellowship with God. He can do these things because God has made him our heavenly Apostle and eternal High Priest.

But there is one vital condition. The text says that Christ is the Apostle and High Priest of our "*confession*". This simply means that Christ will act as your apostle only as you make a right confession of faith. The things that you say, and the way you say them, are the key to this wonderful ministry of Christ.

If you make a good confession, speaking positively and boldly in harmony with the promise of God, then all of the treasures of Christ's apostolic and priestly ministry will be released into your life. But if your confession is wrong, then heaven is free to stay silent and to ignore your prayers.

When he was ministering among the people of Palestine, Christ gave particular attention to this matter of confession. He taught them ....

SPEAK OUT YOUR FAITH IN THE POWER OF GOD

Most people have faith in the power of God, but their faith is vague and uncertain. They know that the Lord governs heaven and earth, that all things are upheld by his power, and that he rules the seasons, the oceans, and the skies. They talk about God as "*the Almighty*", and they have no doubt that he can do whatever he chooses. But all of that is indefinite and far away; for when the matter comes down to their own personal need, their faith begins to shiver and shake and they doubt whether, after all, God can really do anything!

So, the problem people face is not lack of faith in the power of God in a general sense, but rather, in a personal sense. The question you have to answer, then, is not whether God can do anything, but whether he can do this thing, the particular thing you need! It is not a matter of whether all things are possible to God, but whether this thing is possible.

So it is important to believe in the power of God, not just in a vague, general, universal sense, but in a vital, tangible and personal sense. The power of God must cease to be a theory and become a living reality, more real to you than the sin and sickness it opposes.

This is illustrated in the way Jesus dealt with two blind men (Mt 9:28). They came to him crying out for their sight to be restored.

But before Christ made any move to help them he asked, "*Do you believe I am able to do this?*" Only after they replied, "*Yes, Lord!*" did he then say to them, According to your faith, so will it be!" *And at once they received their sight.*

Notice the question Jesus asked.

He did not inquire merely if they had faith in the power of God. He said plainly, "Do you believe that I am able to do this? He wanted them to say, clearly and strongly, that they knew he had power to give them exactly what they asked. He wanted to hear those men actually speak out their confident trust in his power, to say that they were expecting a miracle of healing. Because they did so, their blindness was cured.

In just the same way, Christ wants to hear you speak out boldly your faith in his ability to meet your particular need. If you show the same outspoken boldness those men of old had, his word to you will be as it was to them: "*Your faith has made you whole!*"

SPEAK WITH BOLDNESS

It is obvious that God will only answer prayers that are according to his will. He cannot act against his own character or purpose. Because of this, and because they are ignorant of God's purpose and of his character, many people feel that they should not be too bold in prayer. So they pray hesitantly, and with a show of humble dependence upon God. They bring their petitions to God with trembling uncertainty, and present their requests parcelled and wrapped with an "*if it be thy will*".

You do not often find that kind of praying in scripture. In Bible days people first of all discovered the will of God, and then they were able to pray with fervent passion and with bold strength. And that is the way the Lord Jesus Christ taught us to pray. He said: "*The kingdom of heaven suffers violence, and the violent take it by force*" (Mt 11:12; Lu 16:16).

Do you want to take hold of the blessings and riches, the salvation and healing, the supply and glory of the kingdom of God? Then you will need vigorous faith! You will need to exert some force! Victory goes to the bold! In the words of James -

> *"The fervent and continuous prayer of a righteous man makes tremendous and dynamic power available" (5:16, expanded).*

Prayer is effective when it comes from the depths of your heart, when it is driven by fervent desire, made alive by burning passion! Note what James said. It is not merely the prayer of a righteous man that has great effect, but the fervent prayer. Heaven is moved by a loud cry! Prayer should storm the walls of the kingdom! We are to be like Israel when Joshua commanded the people to SHOUT! Their mighty roar of faith tore down the walls of Jericho!

It is fair to say that this kind of passion in prayer does not always have to be expressed by making a lot of noise. Indeed, you may often speak quietly, and perhaps sometimes not at all. But whether soft or loud, behind your prayer there must be an intensity of purpose that will brook no denial, an exceedingly earnest cry in your heart that clamours for a miracle of God.

Such prayers, when they conform to his will, are irresistible to the Lord. He can do no other than grant your heart's desire. But this is no burden to the Father. He yearns to prosper you more abundantly than you have ever known!

> *"Elijah," we are told, "was a man of like nature with ourselves, and he prayed fervently that it might not rain, and for three years and six months it did not rain on the earth. Then he prayed again and the heaven gave rain, and the earth brought forth its fruit" (Ja 5:17-18).*

Whether you think of that passage as saying that Elijah had the same weaknesses we have, or that we have the same passions Elijah had, its meaning is unchanged: if you will pray as fervently as Elijah did, then God will take as much notice of your voice as he did of the prophet, and stunning things will happen!

Search through the gospels and see how the people prayed who came to Christ for healing. Again and again you will find expressions like "cried out", "begged him", "said with tears", "called loudly", and so on. Those people prayed with energy and with single-minded desire; they called on the Lord with all their heart; they knew exactly what they wanted and resolved to obtain it - and they found their miracle!

SPEAK WITH AUTHORITY AGAINST SATAN

According to scripture, that serpent, Satan, is the source of all our ills. He it is who drives us to sin. He it is who afflicts people young and old with disease. He it is who creates fear, despair, and failure. As Jesus said, Satan is a thief who comes only to steal and to kill and to destroy. But Christ has come that we might have a more abundant life, full of the health, prosperity, and joy of the Lord.

But to gain this full measure of life you must seize your God-given authority and tread underfoot your enemy the devil. The Lord has commissioned you -

> *"Behold, I have given you authority to tread upon serpents and scorpions, and over all the power of the enemy; and nothing shall hurt you" (Lu 10:19).*

The disciples proved the truth of this. Christ sent them out to heal the sick and to set the people free. As they obeyed they found themselves face to face with the devil - for to heal the sick they had to cast out devils (cp. vs 9 with vs 17). When they discovered that Satan was behind disease they gripped the authority Christ had given them, and in the name of Jesus they threw the devils out and healed the people.

When they returned from their mission Christ confirmed the authority he had given them. That same authority belongs now to any who are bold enough to seize it - see Lu 9:49-50. This man had apparently heard Jesus' commission to his disciples and took it as being also valid for him. The Lord acknowledged that he was right!

Notice two things here -

(1) THE ATTITUDE OF CHRIST TOWARD THE FORCES OF SATAN

Serpents and scorpions are noxious, but they are dangerous to us only if we are careless or if we allow ourselves to be paralysed with fear. They are both easily killed. Out in the Australian bush I have killed many snakes and a few scorpions; I am wary of them, but not fearful.

So we should view Satan. If people are careless, or allow terror of his venom to imprison their faith, he may indeed destroy them. Yet he can be overthrown. The Lord declared, "*I saw Satan fall from heaven!*" (Lu 9:18).

(2) THE PROMISE OF CHRIST TO HIS SERVANTS

Jesus made the startling declaration: "*Nothing shall hurt you!*"

That is a sweeping statement.

It does not mean, of course, that no Christian can ever suffer any kind of hurt - Jesus himself was crucified.

But it does mean that you can come to such a place of mastery, through faith, that nothing can touch you except by the express will of God. It does mean that Satan is rendered impotent to hurt you by his own will alone, although God may allow him to stir up men to persecute you for Christ's sake. It does mean that you can find healing and protection against all of the poisons of that wily Serpent.

But all of those things depend upon you courageously seizing the authority Christ has given and confidently stamping the enemy underfoot (cp. Ps 91:13; Ro 16:20).

How can you do that?

Exactly as the disciples did: by a spoken command in the name of Jesus. As Solomon said, "*Surely the serpent will bite without enchantment*" (Ec 10:11, A.V.). So, without the enchantment of the name of Jesus, you have no protection against Satan. But in the name of Jesus you can speak with authority against the devil and all his works.

When you demand that he leave you, he must obey. For the Bible says again: "*Resist the devil and he will flee from you!*" (Ja 4:7).

CONCLUSION

Our text urges us, not only to hold fast to our confession of faith, but also, and most of all, to consider Jesus. That is, fix your eye, your heart, your faith, and your hope solely on Christ. He alone is our High Priest in heaven, who, on the cross, gave his own blood to wash away our sins and to bring us peace with God. He is also our Great Apostle, who brings good news of eternal life, and who alone has power to undo the knots of disease and death and to make us whole.

Keep Christ before you and beside you every step of the way. Be bold to confess your faith in his power. Pray with fervour. Resist Satan with authority. Those are foundations upon which you can build marvellous success in prayer.

CHAPTER SEVEN:

THE NAME OF JESUS

I have three names, two of them given, and a surname: Kenneth David Chant. Those names have a meaning: "*Kenneth David*" (according to some sources) means "*Beloved Leader*", while "*Chant*" has a French origin, and is associated with song. Put them together, and you could call me "*Popular Choir Conductor!*"

Fortunately, however, no one takes any notice of the original sense of my names; such meanings have a curiosity value only. For us, names are a social and legal device, a matter of mere convenience and custom.

But that was not so in Bible days. A name for those people was not just a useful way of distinguishing one person from another. On the contrary, names were intimately associated with their bearers, not just legally, but also in matters of character and position.

The Hebrews attached a mystical significance to a person's name; character and name were thought to strongly influence each other. The name and the person were so closely identified that the two often became inseparable (1 Sa 25:25). Call a man "*Fool*" and he became a fool. His name had power to shape his destiny, to determine his character, to define his nature.

Even existence itself was dependent upon the survival of one's name. To destroy the name was tantamount to destroying the person who bore it (Jb 18:17; 24:20; Ps 109:13; Pr 10:7); and conversely, to preserve the name was to preserve the person who bore it. The person was concentrated in his name. Hence scripture often speaks about the names of the righteous being honoured and preserved, which meant the preservation and honour of the righteous (Ps 72:17).

For such reasons, great importance was attached to the giving of names (Ge 2:19-20; 4:1; 25:25-26; etc.). The name given to a child might reflect the circumstances of his birth, or express the parents' prayer for their child, or indicate the position in life he was expected to hold, or be a prophecy of what he might become, or of events that might be associated with him. But whatever form the name took, it was more than just a conventional appellation; always there was the idea that the name exercised a mystical influence, that it was integrally linked with the destiny of the person who bore it, that his character and personality were present in his name and would be shaped by it.

If a person's status or relationships changed, the name might be changed so that it would better reflect the altered situation. Hence Abram was changed to Abraham (Father of a Multitude), and Sarai to Sarah (to mark an appearance by God), and Jacob to Israel (God Strives), and Solomon to Jedidiah (Beloved by God), and Simon to Peter (a Stone), and Saul to Paul (to mark his commission as apostle to the gentiles).

GOD AND HIS NAME ARE ONE

This identification between a name and the person who bears it was carried over into the way the Hebrews thought about God, but with one major difference: the alliance between an ordinary man and his name often collapsed - he might fail to live up to his name, or the name might fail to exercise its expected influence over him; but no such discrepancy ever arose in the case of the divine name.

God and his name are identical.

The name is God. That is, the Person, Presence, and Power of God are expressed through and revealed by his name. To come to the Name of the Lord is to come into the presence of the Lord himself: " *... all nations shall gather ... to the presence (literally, `the name') of the Lord*" (Je 3:17).

To curse the Name is to curse God:

> *"(He) blasphemed the Name, and cursed ... And the Lord said to Moses, ... `Whoever curses his God shall bear his sin. He who blasphemes the Name of the Lord shall be put to death ... The sojourner as well as the native, when he blasphemes the Name shall be put to death.'" (Le 24:10-16).*

Conversely, to praise the name of God is to praise God himself, for the essence of God is incorporated into his name:

> *"I will give to the Lord the thanks due to his righteousness, and I will sing praise to the name of the Lord, the Most High" (Ps 7:17).*

To know the name of God is to know God. To trust in the name of God is to trust the Lord himself:

> *"Those who know thy name put their trust in thee, for thou, O Lord, hast not forsaken those who seek thee" (9:10) ... "Sing the glory of his name; give to him glorious praise" (66:2).*

Because of this intricate link between God and his name, the OT scriptures affirm that -

(1)THE NAME OF GOD OFFERS THE SAME PROTECTION AND DEFENCE AS IF GOD HIMSELF WERE PRESENT

> *"Our help is in the name of the Lord, who made heaven and earth" (Ps 124:8) ... "Save me, O God, by thy name, and vindicate me by thy might" (54:1) ... "The Lord answer you in the day of trouble! The name of the God of Jacob protect you!" (20:1) ... "I will make them strong in the Lord and they shall glory in his name, says the Lord" (Zc 10:12) ... "I will protect him, because he knows my name" (Ps 91:14) "boast of the name of the Lord our God. They will collapse and fall; but we shall rise and*

stand upright!" (20:7-8) ... "They shall seek refuge in the name of the Lord" (Zp 3:12).

(2)TO ACT IN THE NAME OF GOD IS TO TAKE HOLD OF THE PRESENCE, POWER, STRENGTH, COURAGE, AND RESOURCES OF GOD HIMSELF

God is present in his name. To hold the Name is to hold God. To speak in the Name is to speak with the authority of God -

> *"The name of the Lord is a strong tower; the righteous man runs into it and is safe" (Pr 18:10) ... "Behold, the name of the Lord comes from far, burning with his anger, and in thick rising smoke; his lips are full of indignation, and his tongue is like a devouring fire" (Is 30:27).*

Enemies could be overcome by the power of the name -

> *"Through thee we push down our foes; through thy name we tread down our assailants" (Ps 44:5) ... "For not in my bow do I trust, nor can my sword save me. But thou has saved us from our foes ... and we will give thanks to thy name for ever" (vs. 6,8).*

Such verses clearly show the affinity between God and his name. To conquer by the strength of God is in fact to conquer by his name. To give thanks to his name for victory is to give thanks to God. To bring the name of God against an enemy is to bring God himself into the battle.

(3) PRAISE, JOY, AND WORSHIP ALL SPRING FROM HIS NAME

> *"I will wait for thy name, for it is good, in the presence of the godly" (Ps 52:9, lit.)*
>
> *... "I will bless thee as long as I live; I will lift up my hands and call on thy name" (63:4) ...*

Those who revere the name of God, and who speak it in prayer, will find that God is present with them:

> *"Turn to me and be gracious to me, as is thy wont toward those who love thy name" (119:132) ...*

The name of the Lord is "*near*", and it creates "*wondrous deeds*" for those who embrace it with thanksgiving (75:1, lit.).

Hence those who know the name of the Lord will glory in it, and they will praise the name of God as they would the Lord himself. His name is the source of their gladness, as it is also the object of their praise. They give thanks to his name, and receive joy from it as they would from God:

> *"Yes, our heart is glad in him, because we trust in his holy name" ... "Bless the Lord, O my soul; and all that is within me, bless his holy name ... who forgives all your iniquity, who heals all your diseases" ... "Glory in his holy name; let the hearts of those who seek the Lord rejoice!" ... "I give thanks to thee, O Lord my God, with my whole heart, and I will glorify thy name for ever" (33:21; 103:1; 105:3; 86:12).*

(4) THE NAME OF GOD POSSESSES ALL THE STRENGTH OF GOD

> *"There is none like thee, O Lord; thou art great, and thy name is great in might" (Je 10:6).*

Hence the psalmist is able to affirm that the two greatest things in the universe are the name and the word of God -

> *"I give thanks to thy name ... for thou hast exalted above everything thy name and thy word (138:2).*

The name of God and the word of God hold this place of highest honour for the same reason: God is present in them both. To go with the word of God and to act in the name of God is to take with you all of the invincible might of heaven.

Under those circumstances the next statement is inevitable:

> *"On the day I called, thou didst answer me; my strength of soul thou didst increase" (vs. 3).*

Small wonder that he then sings -

> *"O give thanks to the Lord, call on his name, make known his deeds among the people" (105:1)*

Exciting displays of divine power and provision must attend those who call upon the name of the Lord! But that very fact makes it imperative to approach his name with deep reverence, to utter it with care and with a heart of trust -

> *"Unite my heart to fear thy name ... and I will glorify thy name for ever" (86:11-12).*

This remarkable Hebrew concept of the identification of power with a name is shown by the question the Jewish rulers put to Peter.

> *"By what power or by what name did you do this?" (Ac 4:7).*

They were demanding whether Peter had healed the crippled man by his own personal power, or by power conveyed through the use of a particular name. Peter answered both questions emphatically. He disavowed any personal power, and he said,

> *"(You ask) by what means this man has been healed? Be it known to you all that by the name of Jesus Christ of Nazareth this man is standing before you well!" (vs. 9-10).*

The same principle is seen in Ac 26:9,

> *"I myself was convinced that I ought to do many things in opposing the name of Jesus of Nazareth."*

Thus, to oppose his name was to oppose Jesus himself. His name comprehended all that Jesus represented, it was the embodiment of his doctrines, his character, and his power.

By contrast, to embrace his name was to ally oneself with all that Jesus is, to become united with him and with all of his resources, to assume his character, and to become identified with his person. This use of the resources and power of the name of Jesus is the theme we shall now study . . .

THE NAME OF JESUS

The way in which the NT refers to the name of Jesus exactly parallels the concepts of the OT. Christ is identified with his name. His name is to be praised. His presence and strength are inextricably mingled with his name. All that Jesus is, his name is. The full authority of Christ is vested in his name, and all of his power adheres to it. To honour his name is to honour Christ. To dishonour his name is to dishonour Christ. What is done to his name is as though it were done to the Lord himself.

Christians may take the name of Jesus, and as they speak and act in his name it is as though Christ himself were speaking and acting. They are to go into all the world in his name, and as they do so he will go with them, in association with his name, until this age comes to its end. Through his name all authority in heaven and in earth is made available to the church (Mt 28:18- 20). In his name they are to heal the sick and cast out devils and to act in the full strength of the kingdom of God (Mk 16:16- 20).

All that is inherent in the name of Jesus belongs to the church, for Christ has given us full rights to the use of his name. Possessing his name we possess more than the disciples had when Jesus was living in Palestine, for his physical presence with them was necessarily limited; but his name is now available to every believer, at any time and in any circumstance.

His name means instant access to his total wealth and power; his name means instant participation in all that was gained for the church by his life, death, and resurrection. He is with the church through the strength and authority of his name -

> *"Truly, truly, I say to you, if you ask anything of the Father, he will give it to you in my name. Hitherto you have asked nothing in my name; ask and you will receive, that your joy may be full ... Whatever you ask in my name, I will do it, that the Father may be glorified in the Son; if you ask anything in my name, I will do it ... Whatever you ask the Father in my name, he will give it to you" (Jn 16:23,24; 14:13,14; 15:16).*

When we pray in Jesus' name it is as though Christ himself were praying. The Father delights to answer such prayers, just as he would if they were actually being presented by his Son. Christ speaks through his name. Those who use his name put themselves in the place of Christ, and their prayer gains the same authority as one spoken by Jesus himself.

Hence the boldness of his promise: "*ask anything ... whatever you ask ... you will receive ... the Father will give it to you.*" He could speak so emphatically because he knew the Father always heard him and always granted his requests (Jn 11:41-42).

Similarly, when his disciples prayed in his name it was as though he himself were praying; the answer therefore was just as sure.

When we speak in the name of Jesus the Father in effect sees and hears his Son; therefore he desires to grant our requests, just as he would if they were actually being spoken by Jesus.

So the possibilities encompassed by the name of Jesus are beyond measure. When Christ says to the church, "*Ask the Father whatever you will in my name,*" it is like giving us a signed cheque on the resources of heaven and telling us to fill it in!

WHY HIS NAME IS GREAT

Paul tells us that the Father has made the name of Jesus greater than any other name in heaven, on earth, or under the earth. His name is now the greatest in the entire universe. Before the name of Jesus every knee of angels, men, and demons must bow, whether willingly or unwillingly (Ph 2:9-10; and see also Ep 1:20-21).

In that passage Paul draws attention to two contrasting aspects of the glory of Christ: there is that which is exalted; and there is that which bows.

Christ himself is exalted to the highest place in the universe and his name is above every name, so that now, at the name of Jesus, every knee must bow and every living thing must acknowledge the superiority of Christ and fall prostrate before him.

Heaven bows before that name: which is to say that the servants of heaven hasten to answer the prayers and to do the bidding of those who speak in that glorious name (He 2:13-14).

Earth bows before that name: which is to say that under the impact of the mighty name of Jesus sickness will yield, circumstances will change, mountains will move, victories will be wrought.

Hell bows before that name: which is to say that no demon can withstand the authority of that name, nor can any sin, nor any other thing that originates in the kingdom of darkness.

Ultimately everything must yield before the name of Jesus. That name is invincible and irresistible.

Why has such glorious honour come to the name of Jesus? It is because of his stupendous victory over death - a victory wrought out of his unbroken righteousness -

> *"As to his human nature (Christ) was a descendant of David; but through the Spirit of holiness he has now been declared to be the Son of God with power by his resurrection from the dead: Jesus Christ our Lord!" (Ro 1:4)*

The significance of this to us is that the name of Jesus takes the place on earth of our now ascended and glorified Lord. His name is to us all that he himself would be if he were to come down to earth again, or if we were to rise up to heaven.

If you can place a limit on the wealth and power of the glorified Christ, then you will be able to measure the glory of his name. But who save the Father can compass such majesty? We can hardly begin even to imagine the endless and incredible resources that are now Christ's! There is no authority higher than his. There is no power greater than his. There is no wealth comparable to his. There is no right exceeding his. To think of Christ is to think of the strongest, the wisest, the holiest, the nearest, the highest, the richest! And all that belongs to him belongs to his name. All that he is and all that he has is given to his name - and his name is given to the church!

Christ went to the cross to do battle with Satan. He intended to crush the powers of darkness. He surrendered himself to death as a necessary part of that dreadful conflict.

When they saw his dead body being laid in the grave, the hosts of hell believed that a great triumph was theirs, and for a brief span there was cackling joy in the pits of despair.

But then it happened. An event unparalleled in the history of the universe. Suddenly, savagely, the once-dead man shook himself. Furiously he cast off the confining chains of mortality. He reached out in limitless strength and snatched to himself the gift of divine life. Death cowered away. Its sting was drawn. Its vitality was exhausted. No longer could the pitiless words remain graven on the doors of hades:[9] "*All hope abandon, ye who enter here.*10" The stone had been wrenched away from the Saviour's tomb, and now its open mouth proclaimed endless life to all who believe.

---

[9] Dante, "*Inferno*", Canto 3,50,9

From the winepress of the wrath of God, his garments stained crimson, the great Conqueror strode forth, robed in splendour, glorious in his might.

When they asked him, "Who are you, and why are your garments red?" he replied, "It is I, speaking in righteousness, mighty to save ... I have trodden the winepress alone, from the nations there was no one to help me ... But the day of vengeance was in my heart, and the year of my redemption has come ... So my own arm worked salvation for me, and my own wrath sustained me!" (Is 63:1-5).

Later (in the gospel) he insisted, "No one takes my life from me, but I lay it down of my own accord. I have authority to lay it down, and authority to take it up again!" (Jn 10:18). But demons and men alike mocked him. Such a thing had never been heard before. They thought they had robbed him of life, and mirth filled the hallways of hell as he lay in the cold tomb. But three days later, when he cast off death as a man brushes away a fly and, magnificent in holiness, ascended back to his Father's right hand, a cold shiver of irremediable ruin ran through the dark corridors. Howls of misery sounded in the blackness as a pall of abject and utter defeat fell upon the satanic hordes.

But among men a cry of joy rang out, and the glad news was proclaimed to all who would hear: "The demands of God's offended justice have been met; sin has been requited; death has no more power over this Christ nor over those who call upon his name. Now have come salvation, holiness, victory, and life to all who believe!"

There in the blackness, Jesus had grappled with all of the hideous forces of Satan - the powers of sin, sickness, and death - and he had wrested them out of the devil's hand, and cast his ancient foe aside like a broken twig. Then, tearing his way out of the tomb, so that the very earth quaked, he had risen beyond the boundaries of space and time, to carry his everlasting triumph into the heavenlies.

When they saw him coming, the glittering multitude on the walls of the golden city, raised a thunderous shout: "*Lift up your heads, O you gates; be lifted up, you everlasting doors, that the King of glory may come in!*"

Further back in the City there came a cry: "*Who is he, this King of glory?*"

And the joyous refrain sounded in reply,

> *"The Lord strong and mighty, the Lord mighty in battle, he is the King of glory!" (Ps 24:7-10).*

And as he entered the gates "*he led captives in his train and gave gifts to men*" (Ep 4:8). So the wondering hosts acclaimed his undying supremacy and declared the glory of his name to the furthest reaches of the universe. And the Father also spoke, declaring him to be the Son of God with power, and exalting his name far above every name that has been named.

Now he has given that name to us. It is his greatest gift. He says to you,

> *"Go in my name, and nothing will be able to stand against you. You will tread on serpents and scorpions, and upon all the power of the enemy!" (Mk 16:15-18; Lu 10:18-19).*

All of the authority he so fiercely won, all of the treasures of grace and life he so brilliantly gained, all of the triumph he so superbly wrought, has been delegated to us along with his name. If you hold the Name by faith, then with it you hold all that Jesus is and all that he has.

Those who grip this name need never fear that they can exhaust its potential and bankrupt the Lord it represents! The name is as great as Christ, and Christ is greater than all telling. The more the glories of Christ are studied, the more evident it becomes that in the name of Jesus the church has its greatest resource.

This means you can place the same confidence in his name as you would in Christ himself.

If you have his name you do not need his physical presence, for his name is equivalent to his presence. Whatever you could obtain from the personal or physical presence of Jesus you can obtain from his name. Would Jesus heal you if he walked into your bedroom? Then his name will do likewise. If you could actually see Jesus and talk to him face to face, would you expect a miracle of answered prayer from him? You can expect the same from his name.

That name, the name of Jesus, is as limitless in its power and as inexhaustible in its wealth as Christ himself. All of Christ is in his name. And the Father has given that name to you.

THE USE OF HIS NAME IS DELEGATED TO THE CHURCH

Christ commanded the church to

- go into all the world in his name, and to preach in his name to every nation.
- heal the sick and cast out devils in his name.
- pray in his name.
- command with the authority of God in his name.

He meant that whenever the church found a situation for which its own resources were inadequate, it could confront the problem in his name and at once all that he is would become available. The fullness of the Godhead has been vested in the name of Jesus, and the church has been given the right to draw on that fullness for her every need, by acting in the authority of the Name.

The church can use that name against every foe. By that name we gain free access into the Father's presence. The name of Jesus becomes the cutting edge of bold and exciting prayer that can move mountains and obtain miracles.

All of the omnipotence of God has been joined to the name of Jesus, and if we could learn to use that name with the kind of fearless abandonment the scriptures urge the church to show, then the result would be a thrilling repetition of the Acts of the Apostles!

Yet not even the early disciples managed to do more than begin to develop the latent power of the name of Jesus. The mightiest of God's servants have been able only to touch the shore of the ocean of spiritual power resident in that wonderful name. The best days of the church are still before it as it comes to greater understanding of the measureless wealth God has given it in the name of Jesus!

There are two major grounds upon which the church can build its right to use the name of Jesus

(1)WE ARE BORN INTO THE FAMILY OF GOD, AND HENCE RECEIVE HIS NAME

Have you been born again? Are you a child of God, brought near to him by the blood of the everlasting covenant? Then you have all the right you need to speak and act in the name of Jesus. Since, like Jesus, you are born of the Father you inescapably carry his name. He cannot take that away from you unless you yourself cast it off and take to yourself another name. You are part of his family, and the family name is yours by right. So to you, as well as to every other believer, has been delegated the use of the name of Jesus. This priceless gift, this heavenly authority, has been placed firmly in your hands.

Now you should go in the name of Jesus as he went in the name of his Father. All the power that he had on earth is still with us in his name. Nothing that belongs to the name, or to the One who bears it, has been taken away from you. All that his name holds is yours, and by the name you hold all that belongs to Christ. That name brought down to earth loses nothing of the glory of the Christ who bears it in heaven!

But stand in faith. The name has nothing to offer unbelief. It yields its life and riches only to the believing heart.

(2) THE NAME HAS BEEN CONFERRED UPON US BY CHRIST, ALONG WITH FULL LEGAL RIGHTS TO ITS USE

Note that you actually have a double right to use the name of Jesus. Firstly (as we have just seen), you can claim the name by right of birth into the Father's family. But secondly, you also have a legal right to his name.

If you have been given the legal right to use a person's name, then that name becomes identical with the presence of the person who gave it. You have the same authority as that person, and access to the same resources.

The right to use a name endows you with all of the privileges and entitlements of the actual bearer of the name. It is as if he were with you in person. Those who deal with you must deal with you in the same way as they would with him. If they would obey him, they must obey you. If they would release money for his use, they must do the same for you. If they would honour him, they must honour you. They dare not make any distinction between you and the person in whose name you lawfully present yourself.

The value of the legal right to use a person's name, of course, depends on the position, authority, and wealth of that person. If he is of inferior station, then his name has little worth. But if he is the greatest in the land, then, no matter how humble your personal station might be, his name is a talisman that will open to you all that belongs to your noble benefactor.

A person who ignored his legal right to use a benefactor's great name and tried to present himself in his own unknown name would be foolish indeed. So long as he has the legal right to use the great name he should be glad to do so, and to draw upon all the resources it represents.

Now that describes our relationship to the name of Jesus. Christ has conferred upon his church the legal right to use his name -

> *"Hitherto you have asked nothing in my name; but now you may ask, and you will receive, that your joy may be full ... Truly, truly, I say to you if you ask anything of the Father, he will give it to you in my name" (Jn 16:24,23).*

Those statements convey to the disciples of Christ a legal right to his name. They confer upon us his own authority.

Notice that this right is not based on your personal merit, but on the finished work of Christ at Calvary. You cannot earn or deserve this right. It comes to you as God's free gift. It is based on grace, not works. If you are a child of God through faith in Christ, then you have as much right to use the name of Jesus as the chiefest apostle.

There are two complementary expressions in the NT. The one is "*in Christ*", and the other is "*in his name*". Those two expressions (along with their variants) occur scores of times. The first ("*in Christ*"), describes our legal position, as those who have been justified by faith, who are enthroned with Christ in the heavenlies, who are numbered among the sons of God, who have been given a place in the family of God. The second ("*in his name*"), describes the legal right that this position confers; that is, the right to act as Christ's representatives, to speak with his authority, to claim all of the privileges, power, and wealth inherent in his name.

The first person in history to recognise this legal right, and to act on it, was that remarkable man described by Mark -

> *"John came to Jesus and said to him, `Teacher, we saw a man casting out demons in your name, and we forbade him, because he was not following us.' But Jesus said, "Do not forbid him; for no one who does a mighty work in my name will be able soon after to speak evil of me" (9:38-39).*

Whoever that stranger was, his perception at that time was far in advance of the disciples, and of many church leaders today. He recognised the power and authority belonging to Jesus. He understood that Jesus' name held all that was possessed by Christ himself. He saw that the name would carry the authority of Christ for any person who took hold of it and used it for the glory of God. He understood that this was a legal matter, that it did not depend upon his own good character, but on the strength vested in the name itself. He rebuked demons in that name, and they were compelled to obey him - not because they knew him, but because they knew that name, and they dared not resist it!

Notice also that he had received no special or personal mandate from Christ to heal the sick and cast out devils. As far as I can tell, he never once spoke to Jesus. He had perhaps seen and heard the Lord only from a distance. No angel appeared to him. He had no midnight dream, nor any dawn vision. He apparently had only one thing: he recognised the authority of the name of Jesus, and he knew that all of the power of that name would be his as he spoke it against the devil.

In other words, his position was identical with that of a Christian today - except we have the added advantage of knowing just who Jesus really was, and of being witnesses of his death, resurrection, and ascension. It ought to be much easier for us to believe in and to use the name of Jesus than it was for that stranger!

He watched Jesus give the disciples the right to heal the sick and cast out devils in his name, and he knew at once that this right could not be restricted just to them. If those twelve men could receive authority to speak and act in the name of Jesus, then any of God's servants could assume the same authority. He asked no-one's permission. He made no effort to get into some mystical place of "*holiness*". It does not appear that he spent a long time in prayer and fasting, or in doing anything else. He simply saw that the power of that name did not depend on the virtue of the person who was using it, but on the virtue of Christ.

Modern Christians elevate the apostles to an imaginary place of sanctity and personal merit; but that stranger was certainly not so misled. He saw Peter, John, and the others healing the sick and casting out devils in Jesus' name, and he knew that they were just ordinary men, and that they had no virtue beyond his, nor any access to God better than his. He reasoned that if the name of Jesus had miracle-working power on the lips of Peter, it would have the same power when spoken by him. His assumption was correct. He spoke, and demons cowered before him and were driven out.

The disciples were offended. They no doubt felt at that time (their understanding improved later!) that they were specially chosen by Christ, and that they had a unique claim upon the name of Jesus. They have many supporters today who are still saying the same thing - that the name of Jesus had miracle-working power only for the first apostles.

But Jesus rebuked his disciples - and by inference all who endorse their argument - and made it clear that his name was freely given to the whole church.

It still has the same power on the lips of the humblest servant of God as it does when spoken by the chiefest of them.

You do not need a special mandate from Christ. You do not need personal authorisation. Like that stranger, you can understand what lies behind the name of Jesus, you can accept your legal right to speak and act in his name, and you can begin to take authority over sickness and demons, and to appropriate all that belongs to his exalted name.

The disciples may have been tardy to recognise the full ramifications of their legal right to use the name of Jesus; but after the day of Pentecost they and the whole church with them used that matchless name with stunning boldness and amazing effect - see Ac 3:6,16; 4:7,10,12,17-18,29-30.

But perhaps the most arresting reference is this: "*Philip preached the good news about the kingdom of God and the name of Jesus Christ*" (Ac 8:12). Notice that there were two parts to the message of the early church: they preached about the kingdom of God; and they preached about the name of Jesus.

They had a doctrine of the kingdom, and a doctrine of the name.

Many churches today preach about the kingdom of God, but how many still hold to a clearly defined message about the name of Jesus?

Yet it is evident that preaching about the name of Jesus held a place of high importance in the early church.

Notice also that Philip was not an apostle. He was originally appointed to serve the church in Jerusalem in practical matters (Ac 6:5). But he was driven out of Jerusalem during the persecution stirred up by Saul (8:3-5), and he went down to Samaria and began to preach Christ to the people there. And as he preached he also proclaimed the power of Jesus' name, and in that name he wrought many signs and miracles (vs. 6-8).

And what he did was being done also by other Christians who had been forced to flee from Jerusalem (vs.4). Although Luke does not specifically say that they worked miracles in the name of Jesus, it may be assumed that they did so, just as it may be assumed that Philip continued to do so, although Luke gives no report of it (vs.40).

This much is evident, then: that the early church had formulated a body of doctrine concerning the name of Jesus; that this comprised a very important part of their preaching; that the essence of this doctrine was that the power of Christ was vested in his name; and that the legal right to use it belonged to every member of the church.

Here is another verse that highlights the separate place the name of Jesus had in the preaching and faith of the early church -

> *"This is his commandment that we should believe in the name of his Son Jesus Christ, and love one another, just as he has commanded us" (1 Jn 3:23).*

So there are two things God has commanded us: love each other; believe in the name of Jesus. To believe in the name of Jesus is to believe all that scripture teaches about the name - its identity with the Christ who bears it, its exalted position, its authority and power, the place it holds in the heart of the Father, the legal right each believer has to use that name, and so on.

Thus it is clear from the NT that every believer has been given the legal right to pray in the name of Jesus, and to gain from that Name all of the wealth that is part of our redemption. That Name is love, victory, freedom, healing, pardon, deliverance, joy, and abundant supply. There is nothing lacking from the Name. If you understand the treasure it represents, then you may boldly take from it all that you need.

To the early church that Name meant free access to God, it meant spiritual power, it meant deliverance from their enemies, it meant miracles, signs, and wonders, it meant the mighty power of God at work among them. There is no reason why the name of Jesus should not represent exactly the same to you today.

Let us summarise what we have seen thus far.

To act "*in the name of Jesus*" is to stand in the place of Christ, to act as his representative, to take up his full authority, to do as he would do, and to triumph as he would triumph.

When he gave you the right to use his name he gave you the same access to the Father that he himself has, he gave you the same legal standing he himself possesses. You take his place on earth. You gain his authority in heaven. "*As he is, so are we in this present world*" (1 Jn 4:17).

By his name you gain all the might he has over sickness, demons, and sin. All of the access he has to finance and to abundant supply, you also now have in his name (Mt 17:27; 6:31-33; Lu 9:12-17.)

Notice in that last reference, Jesus told his disciples, "*You give them something to eat!*" In effect he was saying that they could have acted in his name to feed the crowd by a miracle, just as he did.

Entrusted to the name of Jesus are the limitless resources of the mighty God. It is the greatest power given to the church. All that God desires to give us - salvation, healing, the fullness of the Spirit, abundant life, worship, joy, power, authority - comes to us in that wonderful Name!

THE TREASURES OF THE NAME OF JESUS

SALVATION BY HIS NAME

> *When Peter was defending his life against the charges of the Jewish rulers, he boldly cried, "There is salvation in no one else, for there is no other name under heaven given among men by which we must be saved" (Ac 4:12).*

We see at once that the name of Jesus was exclusive - it is the only name that gives access to the salvation of God. No one can come to God, nor find salvation, by any other name. Then we see that it is imperative - by this name men must be saved. If they do not find salvation by calling upon the name of Jesus they will inescapably perish. Again, his name is inclusive - it is given to men, all men; and by it whoever will may come to God freely and find pardon and everlasting life. And it is effective - for it is heavenly in origin. Behind the name of Jesus lies a mighty mandate. By an immutable decree God has sworn that whoever comes to him in the name of Jesus will be adopted into the Father's family, and will receive an eternal inheritance as a child of God.

No one can enter heaven by his own name, nor by the name of a church, nor by any other name under heaven. There is one password alone that promises admission into the mansions on high: JESUS!

At the very beginning of the gospel, salvation was linked with the name of Jesus: "You shall call his name Jesus, for he will save his people from their sins" (Mt 1:21) ... "You shall call his name Jesus. He will be great, and will be called the Son of the Most High ... and of his kingdom there will be no end" (Lu 4:31:33).

From that day there has been no other name so sweet to the repentant sinner. No other balm for sin has ever been found like the name of Jesus. It provides an instant remedy for guilt, an immediate victory over condemnation, an instantaneous release from the fear of judgment.

The prophets of old knew that salvation belonged to the name of the Lord:

> *"It shall come to pass that all who call upon the name of the Lord shall be delivered" (Jl 2:32) ... "He sent redemption to his people; he has commanded his covenant for ever. Holy and terrible is his name!" (Ps 111:9) ... "For God will save Zion ... and those who love his name shall dwell in it" (69:36).*

Isaiah explicitly links a glad experience of salvation with faith in the name of the Lord:

> *"With joy you will draw water from the wells of salvation. And you will say in that day: `Give thanks to the Lord, call upon his name ... proclaim that his name is exalted'" (12:3).*

The apostles quoted the prophets, and emphatically declared that Jesus is the Lord in whose name salvation is found. So Peter applies the words of Joel to Christ:

> *"And it shall be that whoever calls on the name of the Lord shall be saved" (Ac 2:21).*

With even greater boldness he later asserted that all of the prophets had testified that

> *"every one who believes in Jesus receives forgiveness of sins through his name" (10:43).*

But in this he was doing no more than repeating the words of Jesus himself:

> *"Thus it is written, that the Christ should suffer and on the third day rise from the dead, and that repentance and forgiveness of sins should be preached in his name to all nations" (Lu 24:47).*

Now we have discovered the source of the power of the name of Jesus: it was born in his sufferings and came to fullness of might through his resurrection.

The early church understood this, and without hesitation they spoke about it to rulers and people alike.

Thus when Peter and John brought healing to the crippled man in Jerusalem, they preached to the great crowd that gathered:

> *"God has glorified his servant Jesus, whom you gave to Pilate to be killed ... You killed the Author of life, but God has raised him from the dead ... And now his name, by faith in his name, has made this man strong, whom you see and know." (4:8-12)*

The next day, Peter was brought before the Jewish rulers to explain to them what had happened. But none of their threats could deter him from expressing thrilling confidence in the power of the Name, nor from affirming that this name gained its power from the death and resurrection of Christ:

> *"Rulers of the people whom you crucified, whom God raised from the dead, by him this man is standing before you well ... And there is salvation in no other name" (4:8-12).*

At Calvary, Christ submitted himself to the dread darkness of sin, he embraced all of the horror of disease and death, he plunged into the deepest hell - but then, having broken the bands of death, he returned in triumph, stepped out of the tomb and ascended back into heaven, to take his seat at the right hand of the Majesty on high.

In honour of this staggering achievement the Father has decreed that everything in heaven, on earth, and in hell, must bow before the name of Jesus. Nothing can withstand the strength of that name. Sin must yield before that name. Sickness must vanish in the presence of the name. Not even death can imprison those who cry the name of Jesus!

That is why Peter was able to speak in the name of Jesus, and a helplessly crippled man was healed and filled with the joy of God. No other name could have wrought so well. If instead of "*rise in the name of Jesus,*" Peter had said, "*Rise in the name of Moses ... Abraham ... Jerusalem ... Caesar ... (or any other name),*" the cripple would have sat there motionless, impotent.

But the name of Jesus is alive with the resurrection life of the Christ who bears it. As soon as that name was spoken, the strength of God poured from it into the cripple and he was delivered, made well physically and spiritually.

That name has lost none of its efficacy. It is as powerful now as it was then. There is still no other name by which we can find the salvation and healing of God!

All who believe in his name still receive power to become the sons of God (Jn 1:12). Those who do not believe in his name cannot escape the judgment of God, for his name alone can provide security in that day (3:18).

But we who believe are

> *"justified in the name of the Lord Jesus and in the Spirit of our God" (1 Co 6:11).*

The promise is sure:

> *"These are written that you may believe that Jesus is the Christ, the Son of God, and that believing you may have life in his name" (Jn 20:21; 1 Jn 5:13).*

There is life in the name of Jesus! Life greater than all your sin! Life greater than all your sickness! Life tougher than death! Life waiting to spring forth for the benefit of anyone who seizes that name in faith!

You are most certainly included in the promise.

The full salvation of God is proffered to every person who takes hold of the name of Jesus. There is no restriction of person, time, or place. That name is the same for you as it was for the early church or has ever been for anyone:

> *"The same Lord is Lord of all and bestows his riches upon all who call upon him. For, `everyone who calls upon the name of the Lord will be saved'" (Ro 10:13).*

HEALING BY HIS NAME

What I have just written about salvation is equally true of healing. As I have shown in the unit "*Healing In The Whole Bible,*" the words for "*salvation*" and "*healing*" are usually interchangeable in the Greek. So when scripture says "*everyone who calls upon the name of the Lord will be saved,*" it is also saying, "*everyone who calls upon the name of the Lord will be healed.*"

The name of Jesus has lost none of the power Jesus himself had when he was healing vast crowds of sick people by the shores of Galilee. What he was, his name is. As they touched Jesus himself and found healing, so we can hold his name and discover the same miracles. Any afflicted person who brings the name of Jesus against an infirmity, will discover in that name the presence and power of the Great Physician.

The most vivid portrayal of the healing power of the name of Jesus is given in the story of the crippled man who sat by the Beautiful

Gate of the temple - see Ac 3:1-16; 4:5-12. Peter and John used only the name of Jesus to make that man, who had been crippled more than forty years, perfectly whole:

> *"Peter said, `I have no silver and gold, but I give you what I have; in the name of Jesus Christ of Nazareth, walk.' And he took him by the right hand and raised him up; and immediately his feet and ankles were made strong. And leaping up he stood and walked and entered the temple with them, walking and leaping and praising God."*

THIS STORY SHOWS THAT THE NAME OF JESUS EFFECTS HEALING IN THREE WAYS -

(a) His name awakens faith

> *"The name of Jesus, by awakening faith, has strengthened this man ... and this faith has made him completely well" (3:16. NEB).*

No other palliative for unbelief can compare with the name of Jesus, saving the word of God (which stands equal with it in honour - Ps 138:2). There is an amazing dynamic in that name to dispel fear, to arouse hope, to stir faith, and to cause the soul to leap with joy as it grasps the promise of God.

That name awakens faith because of the nature and works of the Man who bears it. If people speak his name carelessly, blaspheming it, unaware of its power, they do so because they have never contemplated Christ. To understand who Jesus is, to know his promise, to recognise his power, is to realise the awesome potential of his wonderful name. The more deeply a person appreciates Jesus, the more mightily his name will awaken faith.

Those who love Christ, love his name. They rejoice in their perception that all that Jesus is belongs to his name. They act in his name as boldly as if Christ were acting in their place. When they go against sickness in his name they know that the Great Physician himself goes with them with his hand outstretched to heal.

(b) Faith is required in his name

> *"Men of Israel, why do you wonder at this, or why do you stare at us, as though by our own power or piety we have made this cripple walk?" (3:12).*

This ends the controversy about the apostles having some special power. Contrary to the opinion of many people today, Peter did not have a unique personal mandate to heal the sick. He firmly denied any unusual degree of "*power or piety*". He would have rebuked those people today who look upon the apostles with a kind of holy awe, who venerate them as possessors of a sanctity not available to ordinary men. He would have been dismayed by any attempt to paint him with a halo. He emphatically declared that he had no extra degree of power, no extra measure of holiness, beyond what is available to any sincere believer.

What then did he have? One thing only: faith in the name of Jesus.

He said,

> *"The name of Jesus, by faith in his name, has made this man strong whom you see and know; and the faith which is through Jesus has given the man this perfect health in the presence of you all" (vs.16).*

He told the people also that the name of Jesus gained its power from the death and resurrection of the Christ who bore it:

> *"What God foretold by the mouth of all the prophets, that his Christ should suffer, he thus fulfilled ... the Christ appointed for you (is) Jesus" (vs. 17-20). And he repeated the same things the next day to the rulers of the city: "By the name of Jesus Christ of Nazareth, whom you crucified, whom God raised from the dead, by him this man is standing before you well" (4:10).*

Language could hardly be plainer!

A cripple was healed simply by speaking the name of Jesus in faith. The man who spoke happened to be the apostle Peter; but he firmly denied that anything in him gave to the name of Jesus added efficacy. That name had power, not because it was spoken by an apostle, but because the man who spoke it believed in it! He did not say, "*I am an apostle, and I have a special right from God to heal the sick in the name of Jesus.*" He did not claim that the name of Jesus had power only when spoken by an apostle. He asserted that it had power for one reason only: he (Peter) had faith in that name!

Surely these things can mean no less than that this name will have the same power for any person who places in it the same faith? The power of the name is released by faith, not by personal sanctity. And faith is not a privilege restricted to apostles. It is universally available to all of the people of God.

So if Peter, through faith in the name of Jesus, could bring healing to the sick, then so may any other servant of God.

You will gain mastery over sickness, for yourself and on behalf of others, not when you achieve some mysterious level of piety and spiritual power, but when you truly believe in the limitless healing virtue of the name of Jesus. Thus James was able to urge the church to grasp the name of Jesus, and to take it boldly against every kind of disease -

> *"Is any among you sick? Let him call for the elders of the church, and let them pray over him, anointing him with oil in the name of the Lord; and the prayer of faith will heal (lit.) the sick man, and the Lord will raise him up" (5:14- 15).*

If those elders could bring healing to the sick by speaking the name of Jesus in prayer, and with faith, so can any of God's people today. The healing virtue was not in the elders, but in the name!

(c) His name is the channel of healing

Peter affirmed that healing came to the cripple -

- by faith in the name of Jesus; and ...
- by the name of Jesus itself.

This name, then, is not only the source of faith, it is also the medicine faith applies to disease.

When there is faith in the name of Jesus, that name becomes the greatest healing power in the world.

Peter had no material wealth, but he did have one magnificent treasure, the name of Jesus:

> *"I have no silver and gold, but I give you what I have; in the name of Jesus Christ of Nazareth, walk" (Ac 3:6).*

He had something. He knew what he had. He knew what the thing he had could do.

Do you have the name of Jesus? Do you know what that name is? Do you understand what it can do?

This name is the real wealth of the church. With this name it is stunningly rich; without this name it is abysmally poor. If the church can say, "*I have silver and gold,*" but cannot say, "*In the name of Jesus stand up and walk,*" then it is utterly impoverished. But though it may lack every material asset, if the church can take hold of the name of Jesus so that it has power to heal the sick and cast out devils, then it is immeasurably rich.

Peter recognised that the name of Jesus is synonymous with healing. He understood that this name was given to him so that by it he could give healing to the sick. If the church is no longer a place of healing, this simply shows that Christians no longer understand either the nature of the name of Jesus or their legal right to possess and use that name. But where people learn the power of that wonderful name, and how to speak it with authority and faith, then miracles of healing and deliverance inevitably occur.

REVIVAL AND MIRACLES BY HIS NAME

The modern church may be weak in its appreciation of the name of Jesus, but the powers of darkness are as fearful of that name as ever they were. From the beginning Satan has recognised that he can destroy the church only if he can deprive Christians of the Name.

So he incited his servants to oppose the early church in its use of the Name. They arrested Peter and John, tried them, and then commanded them not to speak or teach at all in the name of Jesus (Ac 4:17-18; see also 5:27-28). Then

> *"they beat them and charged them not to speak in the name of Jesus, and let them go. (But) they left the presence of the council, rejoicing that they were counted worthy to suffer dishonour for the Name" (vs. 40-41).*

Far from being deterred by that devilled persecution, the disciples prayed with increased fervour, "Lord, look upon their threats, and grant to thy servants to speak thy word with all boldness, while thou stretchest out thy hand to heal, and signs and wonders are performed through the name of thy holy servant Jesus" (4:29-30). Their prayer was heard, and "many signs and wonders were done among the people by the hands of the apostles ... (the people) brought the sick and those afflicted with unclean spirits, and they were all healed" (2:43; 5:12-16).

Under the impact of these things the church grew at an incredible pace. On one day 3000 people were added to their number, and on another day several thousand more, until statistics were overwhelmed and Luke had to write,

> *"more than ever believers were added to the Lord, multitudes both of men and women ... and the word*

> *of God increased, and the number of disciples multiplied greatly in Jerusalem, and a great many of the priests were obedient to the faith" (2:41; 4:4; 5:14; 6:7).*

How marvellously they proved the truth of the prediction of the last of the prophets: "For you who fear my name the sun of righteousness will rise, with healing in its wings. You will go forth leaping like calves from the stall. And you will tread down the wicked, for they will be ashes under the soles of your feet, on the day when I act, says the Lord of hosts!" (Ma 4:1- 3).

Through "*the fear of his name*" the Lord acts!

Thus the early church found it. Though many thousands of them were cruelly martyred, they were glad to "*risk their lives for the name of our Lord Jesus Christ*" (Ac 15:26), lit.), for they knew that even in death they triumphed, and that the church of the Name would remain invincible!

The name of Jesus is the single greatest key to genuine spiritual revival. The church that knows the Name cannot possibly fail. It becomes as unconquerable as the Name itself.

If no more than two or three Christians gather in the name of Jesus, Christ himself is at once among them in all of his resurrection power, giving them access to the limitless resources of heaven (Mt 18:19-20).

No wonder Paul commanded,

> *"Whatever you do, in word or deed, do everything in the name of the Lord Jesus, giving thanks to God the Father through him" (Col 3:17).*

To speak in the name of Jesus is to speak with authority. To act in the name of Jesus is to act in the supernatural. The characteristic of people who know the Name, who live it and speak it every day, is joy; they are continually "*giving thanks to God*" for the mighty victories wrought in them and through them by that Name (see also Ep 5:20).

Demons acknowledge the name of Jesus and yield fearfully before it. They do this in submission to Christ's own promise to his disciples:

> *"You will cast out demons in my name" (Mk 16:17).*

Initially, the disciples were astonished at the authority given to them by the name of Jesus (Lu 10:17,

> *"Lord, even the demons are subject to us in thy name!"),*

but then they grew ever more bold and brought deliverance to an ever-increasing number of afflicted people.

How forcefully they commanded the evil spirits to come out! "Paul was annoyed, and turned and said to the spirit, `I charge you in the name of Jesus Christ to come out of her!' And it came out that very hour" (Ac 16:18). That kind of authority is conveyed by no other name. Only in the name of Jesus can the believer exercise such full mastery over the kingdom of darkness.

But notice that the authority of the Name is not released by merely pronouncing the two syllables which compose it. The sons of Sceva tried that, with a sorry result:

> *"The evil spirit answered them, `Jesus I know, and Paul I know; but who are you?' And the man in whom the evil spirit was leaped on them, mastered all of them, and overpowered them, so that they fled out of that house naked and wounded" (19:13-19).*

Paul was known to the demons, and feared by them, because the apostle was himself personally acquainted with the name of Jesus. Paul understood the nature of the power of the Name, and he knew his legal right to use it. The name of Jesus is powerless for those who use it second hand. The use of the name must be linked with surrender to the Lord to whom it belongs, and with faith in its efficacy when spoken by a true servant of God. The demons will know you when you know the Name, and they will fear you as they fear the Name.

That Name must become more real to you than any other possession, as real as it was to Peter when he said, "*I do not have any money; but I do have the name of Jesus!*" And he gave that Name to the cripple in the form of an incredible miracle of healing.

Paul was equally conscious of the awesome strength of that Name when he exorcised the girl at Philippi, and when he pronounced judgment on the man at Corinth. In the latter incident Paul expressed his complete confidence that "*the power of the Lord Jesus*" would travel with his letter, and with the Name, to bring the discipline of God upon the offender (1 Co 5:1-5).

The scriptures speak about "*the fruit of lips that acknowledge his name*" (He 13:15). This "*fruit*" is praise, and it is also prayer; it is salvation, and it is also healing; it is miracles, and it is power over the kingdom of darkness. Lips that acknowledge the name of Jesus speak with an authority that is second only to that of God in heaven, on earth, and in hell.

My prayer for you is that God will give you a revelation of the name of Jesus, so that you understand its glorious majesty and vigorously exercise your legal right to all that it represents. Seize hold of that wonderful Name, and stand in its strength, until every foe is paying tribute to you and you have entered fully into your inheritance in Christ!

CHAPTER EIGHT:

PRAISE POWER

"Let the righteous be joyful;
Let them exult before God;
Let them be jubilant with joy!
Sing to God,
Praises to his name;
Lift up a song to him who rides upon the clouds;
His name is the Lord, exult before him!" (Ps 68:3-4).

What an exuberant passage of scripture! How filled with excitement and gladness!

The psalmist urges his readers to praise God jubilantly, to rejoice before the Lord with singing, and to be exultant before him. There is an infectious extravagance in his language; it is hard not to be caught up and swept along by the swift current of his praise.

His words encapsule one of the most common themes in scripture: PRAISE.

More than 500 times the Bible refers to offering praise to God, or to rejoicing before him, or to giving him thanks. Again and again the command is laid upon the servants of God that they should devote themselves to praising God. No scripture permits a complaint against God. To murmur against him is pungently forbidden. But in all seasons and circumstances, in all times and conditions, without exception, the children of God are exhorted to praise the Lord.

The purpose of this chapter is to explore the reasons why praise is so imperative. You should praise God every day, and in every situation -

BECAUSE PRAISE RELEASES THE POWER OF GOD

A SPIRITUAL LAW

- A Christian who is weak in praise will be weak!
- A silent saint will be emaciated in every other part of his walk with God.
- If Christians lack the strength of God it is because their lips are slack in praise.
- The Christian who is strong in praise will be strong in everything.

In the words of Nehemiah:

> *"The joy of the Lord shall be your strength!" (8:10).*

A spiritual law comes into operation when the servants of God praise their Lord. There is a release of divine power into the heart of true praise. God responds to the praises of his people by granting them the strength they desire. Praise is the key to power!

As the psalmist said: "*Thou hast a mighty arm; strong is thy hand, high thy right hand.*" But who are those favoured people who know the glorious strength of the Lord? For whom is his mighty arm bared? The psalmist answers -

> *"Blessed are the people who know the festal shout ... who exult in thy name all the day, and extol thy righteousness. For thou art the glory of their strength!" (89:13-17).*

They are happy indeed who know how to raise a shout of praise to the Lord, who have discovered how to exult in his name, and for whom the strong hand of God is stretched out in blessing!

If you discover in yourself some desperate weakness, the solution is not to give yourself to bemoaning your infirmity, but rather to give yourself to praising your Creator. You will gain strength as you rejoice in the Lord.

Whenever you find yourself in a situation for which either you or your resources are inadequate, start praising God.

There is no substitute for praise!

Praise is the only possible representation of faith. If you are believing God you will rejoice in God -

> *"Without having seen him you love him; though you do not now see him you believe in him and rejoice with unutterable and exalted joy" (1 Pe 1:8).*

Faith is called for when you cannot see God, when it seems that he has forgotten you, when it appears that ruin is about to overwhelm you. But though we do not see him, nor any of his mighty works, scripture insists that we hold unwaveringly to our faith in his goodness and mercy. And those possessing such faith will surely rejoice in it. With exalted praise they will magnify the Lord. Thus they show the reality of their faith. Thus the power of God will be released into their circumstances.

God has promised that when faith is expressed through exuberant praise he will respond with strength. Nobody can truly praise God and remain weak. Power flows out of praise as surely as heat from a fire.

SUPPORTING REFERENCES

There are many places in scripture where the strength of God is linked with praise, or depicted as flowing out of it -

(1) "The Lord is my strength and my shield; in him my heart trusts; so I am helped, and my heart exults, and with my song I give thanks to him. The Lord is the strength of his people" (Ps 28:7-8).

Those verses show a proper development of faith

- there is a statement of fact: "*The Lord is my strength;*"

- followed by an expression of faith: "*in him my heart trusts;*"
- followed by an inner response of joy: "*my heart exults;*"
- followed by spoken praise: "*I give thanks to him.*"

Faith always begins with a promise of God, then develops into spoken praise, which leads to the fulfilment of the promise. The hiatus between the promise and its fulfilment is always bridged by praise.

(2) "A cheerful heart is a good medicine, but a downcast spirit dries up the bones" (Pr 17:22).

That verse on the surface does no more than describe a fact of ordinary life: a merry heart leads to good health, a miserable spirit brings illness. But at a deeper level it enshrines the spiritual law that praise releases the power of God. It is especially a heart cheerful with the praise of God that is "*good medicine*". It is the joy of the Lord that opens a channel through which his healing grace may flow.

But a downcast heart, one in which unbelief reigns supreme, and in which the voice of praise is silent, brings weakness and defeat.

True faith is demonstrated by lively praise. The believer who is confident that God is in control of his life, who is sure that all things are being ordered by the Lord, will always find cause to rejoice in the Lord. Nothing will be able to still his praise. He cannot doubt that "*God is working in everything for good*" (Ro 8:28), and in that assurance he will be glad in the Lord.

A capacity for joy in every circumstance is one of the chief hallmarks of a true Christian. In life or death, in happiness or sorrow, in pleasure or pain, in wealth or poverty, in ease or difficulty, in the face of petty irritation or of great tragedy, the souls of the righteous can always find a place of jubilation in God.

This ability to be always glad in the Lord sets them apart as the supernatural people of God, a people possessed by the Spirit of

God, a people who cannot help but rejoice because they know themselves to be sufficient for every situation (2 Co 3:4,5; 9:8).

(3) "God is enthroned upon the praises of his people" (Ps 22:3).

Do you want God to act with authority in your life? Do you need his hand to touch your circumstances with power, to bring you a miracle of healing or of divine supply? Then build the King a throne of praise!

The Lord has resolved: "*I will inhabit the praises of my people.*" To those who praise him he is near. From those who praise him not he is distant.

Kings desire thrones, and from those thrones they exercise their royal authority. So your praises are reckoned by the King of kings to be his chief throne. Upon that throne he will take his seat in glorious might and majesty, and from it he will stretch forth his sceptre of salvation and deliverance.

Psalm 22 contains an extraordinary picture of a man who begins with a cry of despair, but who then turns his complaint into praise, and so discovers a great miracle of heaven[11]

His complaint is found in vs. 1-3; his praise in vs. 3-5; his testimony of answered prayer in vs. 22-24. Then he makes a

---

11 I am aware, of course, of the amazing messianic and prophetic character of Psalm 22 (eg, vs. 1, 6-10, 14-18, 27-31), and that the expressions used throughout it cannot reasonably be restricted just to events in the life of David. None-the-less, the initial stimulus for this Psalm seems to have been an occasion when God, after appearing at first to ignore his servant's cries for help (vs. 1-3), finally responded to David's faith with a wonderful answer to prayer (vs. 22-24). The crisis may have been a time of serious illness (vs. 14-15), and it would seem David originally intended to write a poem simply about that personal affliction and deliverance; but the spirit of prophecy seized him and he wrote instead an incredibly accurate prediction of the suffering, death, resurrection, and ultimate triumph of his great Descendant, our Lord Jesus Christ. Nonetheless, David's own experiences clearly provide the underlying base of the prophecy.

statement about the lesson he had learned concerning the power of praise:

> *"From thee comes my praise in the great congregation; my vows I will pay before those who fear him. The afflicted shall eat and be satisfied; those who seek him shall praise the Lord!" (vs. 25-26).*

The underlying sense of these verses is that while it may be legitimate for you to express honestly your doubt, or grief, or even complaint to God, eventually you must turn from such expressions to praise - for the healing grace of God responds only to praise.

The psalmist's affliction was desperate, and his situation tragic (vs. 12-18), but he disciplined his soul to rejoice in the Lord, he took himself to church so that he might join with the people of God in praise (vs. 22), and then he gained the miracle he needed (vs. 23-24).

God will be enthroned in your life as often as you set yourself to praise him, regardless of your circumstances; and your praises will enable him to complete readily all that lies in his program for your life. A dull spirit, one heavy with unbelief, inhibits the flow of divine grace; but a lively heart, continually joyful in the Lord, provides an open channel for a full measure of God's goodness and mercy.

(4) "Let the faithful exult in glory; let them sing for joy on their couches. Let the high praises of God be in their throats, and two edged swords in their hands; to wreak vengeance on the nations ... This is glory for all his faithful ones!" (Ps 149:5-9).

Notice the similarity between the first and the last clauses: "*Let the faithful exult in glory ... This is glory for all his faithful ones.*" Those two statements provide a frame within which the psalmist declares the power of praise. He is saying that the saints should be jubilant in the "*glory*" God has given them.

And what is this "*glory*"?

It is simply that praise renders them invincible against all their foes!

If the "*faithful*" will discipline themselves to exult in the Lord, to sing joyfully to him day and night, to shout the high praises of the Lord, then they will always be armed with the sharp sword of victory: "*This is glory for all his faithful ones!*"

The Hebrew of vs. 6 is quite pungent. It says something like this: "*Let high praises come from deep throats, and many-mouthed swords in their hands.*" High praises, deep throats, many-mouthed swords: what an extraordinary combination! But it vividly describes both the nature and effect of true praise, which comes from deep in the heart, soars high into the heavens, and then arms the believer with weapons that are mighty in God.

There is no room in true praise for shallow repetition (cp. Mt 6:7).

Praise that is nothing more than habitual and careless cliches is not praise. Praise that contains only the same handful of words or phrases, repeated over and over again, is not praise.

True praise arises out of the heart's deep communion with God. It will embrace the full range of God's wondrous works in creation and his dealings with his people. It will be enriched by the imagery, songs, and thanksgivings that abound in scripture. It will involve the worshipper's whole being, body, soul, and spirit. It will be thrust into heaven by faith. It will tell the high glory of God. It will be focussed more on eternal and heavenly things than on things of the earth. It will be spiritual praise. It will arise from a heart open to the guidance and inspiration of the Holy Spirit. It will centre on God himself. It will be rich, lively, and creative.

Such praise, various, rapturous, jubilant, will be like a "*many-mouthed sword.*" It will be an irresistible spiritual weapon, "*having divine power to destroy the strongholds of the enemy*" (2 Co 10:4). It will open a way for the might of the Lord to pour into the worshipper's life.

As Paul says, those who stand in the joy of the Lord, giving thanks to the Father, will be "*strengthened with all power, according to his glorious might*" (Col 1:11-12). In that strength they will gain a mastery over their circumstances that will lead either to a miracle of divine deliverance, or to a miracle of patient endurance.

(5) "Continue steadfastly in prayer., being watchful in it with thanksgiving ... Live in Christ, rooted and built up in him and established in the faith, abounding in thanksgiving ... Have no anxiety about anything, but in everything by prayer and supplication with thanksgiving let your requests be made known to God" (Col. 4:2; 2:7; Ph. 4:6).

"*With thanksgiving*" - those two words make one of the major differences between prayer that is answered and prayer that is not.

But what should you thank God for as you pray, and how should you thank him?

The kind of thanksgiving that can transform flaccid, ineffectual prayer into a thing of dynamic spiritual power will

- praise God for his glory and majesty and for all of his mighty works, in heaven and on earth.
- praise God for his unfailing goodness and love, allowing no room for doubt about his wisdom, nor about his perfect control over every event.
- thank God for the assurance that nothing can happen to his servants that is contrary to his divine purpose, but all things are ordered according to his will.
- rejoice in God's limitless ability to answer every prayer, to solve every difficulty, to meet every need.
- if the prayer is based on a specific word[12] from God, rejoice in the certainty that the miracle is already done, whether or

12 A "*rhema*"; see the DCC unit, "*Faith Dynamics,*" where there is a full discussion of this concept

not there is yet any physical evidence of it (Mk 11:24; Mt 21:22; 1 Jn 5:14-15).

Prayer empty of that kind of thanksgiving is prayer empty of power. It is empty of power because it is evidently empty of faith. Where there is real faith there will be lively praise. Faith and praise are as inseparable as lightning and thunder. The one follows inevitably from the other. Praise is the salt that adds savour to faith. Without praise faith sags into anaemic impotence. But with praise faith sparkles into robust life. Praise is both the expression of faith and its best nourishment.

So if you are believing God you will certainly praise God.

But the converse is also true: if you set yourself to praise God you will soon begin to believe God. It is impossible to truly praise him and at the same time to continue doubting his goodness or his power.

Praise, therefore, is a natural corollary to explosive faith; and it also has the ability to create an explosion of faith. Praise and faith are each the outcome and the forerunner of the other.

Hence Paul says that those who are living in Christ, who are rooted in him, and who are established in the faith, will also "*abound in thanksgiving*" (Col 2:7). They abound in thanksgiving because they are established in faith; they are established in faith because they abound with thanksgiving. Faith and praise follow each other as day follows night, and night follows day.

Praise, then, has power

- to raise the dead (Jn 11:41).
- to smash barriers (Jsh 6:20).
- to bring victory (2 Ch 20:22-23; Jg 7:20-22; 2 Ch 13:13-15).
- to open prisons (Ac 16:25-26).
- to bring healing (Ps 30; 31; 103:1-3).

- to meet every need (Ps 103:4-5; 37:3-5).

But it must be emphasised that praise is effective only when it comes from a sincere heart. The praises of the ungodly, the rebellious, the disobedient, are repulsive to God. So there was an occasion when the Israelites thought they could raise a shout to God and defeat their enemies as they had done before. They shouted until the very earth rang, yet they were savagely mauled by the enemy. They did not realise that because of their sin the glory of God had departed from them (see 1 Sa 4:1-22, especially vs. 5,10,21; see also Jb 20:5; Pr 10:28; 21:13; 28:9).

A person may extol the Lord with his tongue, and raise a vigorous shout of praise, but if he continues to cherish iniquity in his heart the Lord will not listen to him (Ps 66:17-18). Praise is not the mere mouthing of words. It is a joyful cry from the heart.

There are many today who are as sadly deceived as the former citizens of Jerusalem. Because the Temple was thronged with worshippers who intoned the formula, "*The temple of the Lord, the temple of the Lord, the temple of the Lord,*" they thought no army could conquer their city (Je 7:1-4). But their worship was futile and their praise was hollow. The fierce indictment was announced by the Lord -

> *"Behold, you trust in deceptive words to no avail. Will you steal, murder, commit adultery, swear falsely, burn incense to Baal, and go after other gods that you have not known, and then come and stand before me in this house, which is called by my name, and say, `We are delivered!' - only to go on doing all these abominations?"*

That which passes as praise may be no more than "*deceptive words*", a vain ritual repetition, mindless, dull, repulsive to God.

To be meaningful, praise must come from a warm heart and be an expression of obedient worship. Like manna, it must be gathered fresh each day, and presented to God with vitality.

That is why you will find in scripture this frequent exhortation: "*Sing a new song!*" (Ps 33:3; 96:1; 144:9; Is 42:10).

Never allow praise to become routine. Notice how the people of Judah had lapsed into a monotonous incantation of praise, a mere ritual formula: "*The temple of the Lord, the temple of the Lord, the temple of the Lord.*" When praise becomes a hollow rehearsal of the same phrases, over and over again, it has ceased to be praise. There should be a new theme for each new day, a new song for each new situation.

We should be like the psalmist, who found that each time God answered his prayers he had discovered a new way of blessing the Lord -

> *"He drew me up from the desolate pit, out of the miry bog, And set my feet upon a rock, making my steps secure. He put a new song in my mouth, a song of praise to our God!" (40:1-3).*

BECAUSE PRAISE IS AN ACCEPTABLE SACRIFICE

PRAISE IDENTIFIED AS SACRIFICE

There are several places where praise is identified as a proper sacrifice to offer God, but the three following will suffice -

> *"Offer sacrifices of thanksgiving, And tell of his deeds with songs of joy Ps 107:22*

> *"Take with you words and return to the Lord; Say to him, 'Take away all iniquity; Accept that which is good and we will render the fruit of our lips" (Ho 14:2).*

The next passage appears to be drawn from the two above -

> *"Let us continually offer up a sacrifice of praise to God, that is the fruit of lips that acknowledge his name." (He 13:15).*

Each of those references describes praise as a sacrifice offered to God. The words of Hosea are especially vivid. They read literally: "*We will offer the bulls of our lips.*" That is, in place of the flesh of an animal sacrifice, they will offer praise to God. Instead of taking a calf or a lamb to the altar, they will "*take words*", words of penitence, and words of praise.

The psalmist expressed the same idea when he wrote -

> *"I will praise the name of God with a song;*
> *I will magnify him with thanksgiving.*
> *This will please the Lord more than an ox*
> *Or a bull with horns and hoofs" (69:31-32).*

All of those passages recognise that ultimately there is only one sacrifice man can offer God, and that is praise. Our greatest need is praise, for almost every other spiritual advance will result from praise.

Those who offer God generous praise cannot be parsimonious in the other things they give to God. To be released in praise, is to be released in every relationship with God. Those who truly praise the holiness of God cannot easily turn to sin. Praise leads to a holy life. Those who speak their adoration of God, who fill their mouths with words of thanksgiving, whose hearts daily exult in the Lord, will be irresistibly shaped into the likeness of God.

To give God time, money, goods, even your own flesh, but not to give him true praise, is mockery. The prophets all recognised this, and wrote words that must have stunned their original hearers.

Were not the animal sacrifices ordained by God himself? Did he not personally tell Moses how to build the Tabernacle? Did he not himself explicitly detail all of the ordinances and ceremonies that were to control the worship of Israel?

Yet the prophets made arresting statements like these -

> *"I have had enough of burnt offerings of rams and the fat of fed beasts; I do not delight in the blood of bulls, or of lambs, or of he-goats. When you come to appear before me, who requires of you this trampling of my courts? ... Your appointed feasts my soul hates ... If you are willing and obedient you shall eat the good of the land; but if you refuse and rebel you shall be devoured by the sword ... You add your burnt offerings to your sacrifices, and eat the flesh; yet in the day that I brought them out of the land of Egypt, I did not speak to your fathers or command them concerning burnt offerings and sacrifices. But this command I gave them, `Obey my voice, and I will be your God, and you shall be my people' ... He who slaughters an ox is like him who kills a man; he who sacrifices a lamb, like him who breaks a dog's neck ... I hate, I despise your feasts, and I take no delight in your solemn assemblies! (See Is 1:11-15; 66:3; Je 6:20; 7:21-23; Ho 8:13; Am 5:21-23; see also Mi 6:6-8).*

Behind these incredible words is the spiritual law that no sacrifice, or offering, or toil, or worship, or service, has any value to God unless it is motivated and surrounded by genuine, loving, grateful praise. Praise must be the living heartbeat of all that we offer God or do for him.

There is a reason for that law. It is simply this: there is finally only one truly unique gift we can offer God: and that is our praise.

Praise is the only possession we have that is of any value to him. It is the one thing the Father cannot create by his own power nor compel by his own will.

He has no need of your money or your goods. Your labour adds nothing to his wealth. Praise remains the one gift you can present to God that brings both joy to his heart and treasure into heaven.

Especially when that praise is impelled by rapturous love for God, and springs out of trust in his goodness and mercy.

As early as the reign of David, before even the Temple was built, Asaph wrote a vivid poem about this spiritual law (Ps 50). He reminded Israel that God was willing to accept their animal sacrifices, but at heart the Lord was actually indifferent to them. No bull from their house, nor goat from their fold, could really effect any spiritual change in them (vs.7-9). How could they imagine that such offerings had any value for God when he could say, "*Every beast of the forest is mine, and the cattle on a thousand hills*" (vs. 10-11)? Indeed, the world and all that is in it is his! (vs.12). So the Lord demanded: "*Do I eat the flesh of bulls, or drink the blood of goats?*" (vs.13).

What then does God want? What can we give him that will be precious in his sight? What sacrifice will please him?

> *Asaph replied: "Offer to God a sacrifice of thanksgiving, and pay your vows to the Most High ... He who brings thanksgiving as his sacrifice honours the Lord" (vs. 14, 23).*

There is another reason for this spiritual law.

There are basically two kinds of sacrifice men can offer God: a sacrifice to atone for sin; and a sacrifice of thanksgiving -

(1) A SACRIFICE OF ATONEMENT

There is in the heart of man a desire to make some kind of personal atonement for sin; and that desire is matched with a reluctance to accept the sacrifice God has freely provided in Christ. Accordingly, men and women have always sought either to ignore God's provision altogether, or to add something to it. So there are people who have persuaded themselves that if they work hard enough, or give enough money, or show enough charity, or produce enough personal righteousness, God will become obliged to pardon their few sins and welcome them into heaven.

Then there are others who know that they need the Saviour, yet they are not content to trust in him alone. They feel compelled to complete his work of atonement by additional sacrifices of their own.

But the scriptures are emphatic on this point. Either the sinner must trust exclusively in Christ as his sufficient, God-given sacrifice; or he must fall back upon his own wholly inadequate resources, and perish -

> *"Shall I come before God with burnt offerings, with calves a year old? Will the Lord be pleased with thousands of rams, with ten thousands of rivers of oil? Shall I give my first-born for my transgression, the fruit of my body for the sin of my soul? ... For the Lord desires steadfast love and not sacrifice; the knowledge of God, rather than burnt offerings... price of his life, for the ransom of his life is costly, and can never suffice, that he should continue to live on for ever, and never see the pit" (Mi 6:6-8; Ho 6:6; Ps 49:7-8).*

Plainly, there is no gift, or service, or sacrifice that can provide any kind of atonement for sin. Either God himself provides a full and perfect atonement, or we are doomed to fall without remedy into the Pit, forever to lie in chains, forever cut off from God.

Of course, the witness of scripture is that Christ is the Lamb of God, and that by him God has made full atonement for every sin. Those who wish to escape the penalty and power of sin can do so only by placing all of their confidence in the ransom Christ paid with his own blood. He has once for all made the complete sacrifice for sin. We can add nothing to it, nor take anything from it (Mt 20:28; Mk 10:45; 1 Ti 2:6; Ro 3:21-28; Ga 3:1-11).

The true people of God have always recognised that no sacrifice prepared and offered by human hands could ever have any value in atoning for even the most insignificant sins. They have known that only God could provide a ransom for the sin-stained soul, and they have been content to cast themselves upon the mercy of God.

If full pardon does not come to us as a free gift, based on a divinely provided atonement, then it cannot come to us at all, for we have no capacity to pay even a tiny part of the price of God's forgiveness. Nothing we can do, nothing we can offer, can induce God to add anything to the salvation he has freely provided in Christ. He simply demands that we accept salvation as an unqualified gift, or accept it not at all.

Since we cannot offer any kind of atonement-sacrifice to God, there is only one other gift we can offer that has value for him, and that is -

(2) A SACRIFICE OF PRAISE

David understood this principle.

His murder of Uriah, and his adultery with Bathsheba, had been exposed by the prophet Nathan. How could he regain his fellowship with God? How could he obtain God's forgiveness? How could the joy of salvation be restored to him? What labours could he perform, what pains could he endure, what sacrifices could he make?

There were none that were acceptable to God.

He had no choice but to depend utterly upon God's loving kindness and mercy. Therefore he said -

> *"Thou hast no delight in sacrifice; were I to give a burnt offering thou wouldst not be pleased. The sacrifice acceptable to God is a broken spirit; a broken and contrite heart, O God, thou wilt not despise ... O Lord open thou my lips, and my mouth shall show forth thy praise" (Ps 51:16,17,15; see also the remainder of the Psalm).*

The writer to the Hebrews also draws this careful distinction between an atonement-sacrifice, which we cannot offer, and a praise-sacrifice, which we should offer. He declares emphatically that all sin-offerings have been replaced by Christ, who has sanctified us fully by his own blood (He 13:9-12). There now remains to us only the sacrifice of praise (vs.15). Whatever else we do for God, church, and neighbour, ought to be done as an extension of, or an expression of, our loving praise, not as a means of buying salvation.

WHEN DOES PRAISE BECOME SACRIFICIAL?

Now we come to an intriguing question: when is praise a sacrifice? Normally it could be said that "*sacrifice*" is a strange word to link with "*praise*". We usually think of praise as pleasurable rather than painful. It would also be fair to say that praise cannot always be described as a sacrifice. Many times it costs us nothing to praise God. But praise does become a sacrificial offering to God when it assumes one special quality. That is, when it is offered continually.

Many references teach that praise is most honoured by God when it continues through every circumstance -

> *"I will bless the Lord at all timesHis praise shall continually be in my mouth" (Ps 34:1).*
>
> *"My praise is continually of thee ...*
>
> *My mouth is filled with thy praise,And with thy glory all the day ...*
>
> *But I will hope continually ...*
>
> *And I will praise thee yet more and more" (Ps 71:6,8,14).*
>
> *"Every day I will bless thee,And praise thy name for ever and ever" (Ps 145:2).*
>
> *"From the rising of the sun, to its setting, The name of the Lord is to be praised" (Ps 113:3).*

This OT refrain was taken up even more vigorously by the NT writers -

> *"Sing and make melody to the Lord with all your heart, always and for everything giving thanks in the name of our Lord Jesus Christ to God the Father ... Rejoice always, pray constantly, give thanks in all circumstances, for this is the will of God in Christ Jesus for you ... Rejoice in the Lord always; again I will say, Rejoice!" (Ep 5:19-20; 1 Th 5:16-18; Ph 4:4).*

The sense of those exhortations is plain: there is never an occasion that warrants the staunching of praise. Thus we are to rejoice at all times, giving thanks and praising God in every situation. We are to do this because "*this is the will of God*" for each one of his children.

Praise gains its greatest worth when it hurts. The best time to praise God is when you least feel like it.

After all, it is a simple matter to burst into praise when God has given you prosperity and good health, when your prayers are being wonderfully answered, and life is filled with happiness and pleasure. Who would not praise God in such circumstances?

Again, it is easy and delightful to rejoice before the Lord in church, when you are surrounded by the people of God, and carried along with their worship and joy.

But when you are alone, when tragedy is cruelly shattering your happiness, when your dreams have become nightmares, and each new day increases the dolour and misery of the old, how then can the voice of praise sound?

Yet praise deserves the name only when it is offered continually - that is, when it finds its chief motivation in the unchanging God himself, and not in shifting circumstance. We are to rejoice in the Lord, not in the situation. We are to thank God for what he is more than for what he does.

Many people take offence at Paul's demand: "*Always and for everything give thanks to God the Father.*" Is this really possible? Surely there are some conditions where to rejoice would be insensitive, callous, even cruel? Does not scripture itself allow that there are times when tears are more appropriate than laughter? (Ecc 3:4; Ja 5:13; Ps 126:5-6; Jn 16:20; Ro 12:15).

When Paul wrote to the Philippians he anticipated just those kinds of objections. He said to them, "*Rejoice in the Lord always!*" And then, as though he could hear them beginning to protest, he immediately repeated the demand: "*Again I will say, Rejoice!*"

That double emphasis (which is peculiar to this letter) must have reminded the Philippians that Paul was himself a living example of the power of such praise. When he and Silas had been flogged by the rulers of Philippi, and brutally chained to the stocks in the inner prison, what did they do? Bitterly lament at the injustice they had suffered? Complain that God had failed them? Rage against the barbarity of the Romans? Sob with fear and anxiety? Let Luke answer: "*But about midnight, Paul and Silas were praying and singing hymns to God when suddenly there was a great earthquake, so that the foundations of the prison were shaken; and immediately all the doors were opened and everyone's fetters were unfastened*" (Ac 16:22-26).

It cannot be imagined that Paul and Silas were happy because their bodies were bruised and torn by the savage beatings inflicted on them. They could not have wanted their feet to be clamped and stretched in the stocks. The agonies of cramp, of twisted limbs, of battered flesh surely brought them no pleasure. It is almost certain that their faces were drawn with pain, and their eyes awash with tears. They could not have had any natural joy in that prison.

How then could they sing hymns at midnight?

Because they had learned how to find joy in God himself!

No matter how abject their earthly state, nor how bitter their present sorrow, the name of the Lord was still worthy of praise. No matter what else may have been taken from them, the greatest cause of joy remained unharmed: their names were written down in the Book of Life, they were children of the King, they had treasure eternal in heaven (Lu 10:20; 12:32-34).

The children of God always have more on their side than can ever be against them. They always have more wealth than poverty, more strength than weakness, more victory than defeat, more holiness than iniquity, more health than sickness, more life than death. Therefore they always have more cause for joy than they ever have for sorrow. That is why the trusting heart will always seek for a place of delight and praise in God. "*Always, and for everything, and in all circumstances*" the true servant of God will look for a reason to give thanks to God.

For example:

- if you are sorrowful, you could thank God for the consolation Christ gives, and for the opportunity of learning through affliction how to comfort others (2 Co 1:3-5).
- If you are bewildered, you could look past the perplexities of life and rejoice in the assurance that God is working for good in every happening (Ro 8:28).
- If you are in want, your soul could exult in the all-sufficiency of Christ and in the certainty that as you stand firm in faith the Lord will in time meet your every need (Ph 4:11-13, 19-20).
- If you have been defeated, you could praise God for the security you have in the heavenlies in Christ, and for the wisdom of God that can turn even "*the wrath of man*" to good advantage (Ps 76:10; Ep 1:3-7; see also Mi 7:8-10, the testimony of a man who refused to capitulate to his own weakness, who would not accept defeat, who refused to be bowed by his enemy's scorn, who would not even despair

in the face of the indignation of God, but who resolved, come what may, to worship and praise God, vs.7).

- If you are being persecuted, you could find joy in being able to suffer for Christ and in the discovery that the grace of God is sufficient in every trial (Ac 5:40-42; Ro 5:3-5; 2 Co 12:8-10; 1 Pe 4:12-14).

When scripture says "*thank God for everything*", it means that if you look for it you can always find a place of joy in God. In every situation there is always some cause for the Christian to rejoice. By praise each situation is sanctified and turned into a stairway to paradise.

Praise God continually! That demand separates true faith from the spurious. It forbids any murmuring about the providence of God (1 Co 10:9-11; He 3:12-14). It creates a divine solution to the needs of every circumstance. By offering such a sacrifice of praise to God you create a faith environment in which the Holy Spirit has great room to move and to create for you a miracle of answered prayer.

BECAUSE PRAISE BRINGS INCREASE

Scripture indicates that praise is a fruitful field out of which a delightful harvest may spring. Those who praise God will find his blessing pouring upon them

> *"like rain that falls on the mown grass, like showers that water the earth!"*

For them the word will be fulfilled,

> *"May there be abundance of grain in the land; on the tops of the mountains may it wave; may its fruit be like Lebanon" (Ps 72:6.16, with vs. 17-19).*

For them the prophecy will come to pass -

> *"Behold, the days are coming when the ploughman shall overtake the reaper and the treader of grapes him who sows the seed; the mountains shall drip sweet wine, and all the hills shall flow with it" (Am 9:12).*

Praise yields increase in two ways: naturally, and spiritually -

(1) THERE WILL BE NATURAL INCREASE

> *"Let the people praise thee, O God; Let all the people praise thee. Then shall the earth yield her increase; And God, even our own God, shall bless us" (Ps 67:5-6. AV).*

That passage is typical of many that directly link natural increase and prosperity with praise - see also Ps 85:9-12. A promise is given that the Lord will look with favour upon people who set themselves to praise him day by day. He will abundantly answer their prayers and richly meet their physical and material needs. The voice of praise attracts the riches of God, but "*a dumb spirit and a hymnless heart*" closes heaven's storehouse.

Christ recognised this principle when he gave thanks to God before he divided five loaves and two fish into a meal sufficient for 5000 men (Mk 6:41-44). Praise is a key to the supernatural power of God. Praise can turn poverty into plenty. Those who are in want should sing, not sigh; they should laugh, not lament. Praise opens the door to heaven's abundance!

There are, of course, exceptions to this principle, for sometimes God has a purpose for his servants higher than merely granting them material prosperity. I will say more about that in a moment. But it may be generally accepted that God wants you to have good health and prosperity, and that the key to this outer abundance is a prosperous soul (3 Jn.2). And how better can the soul show its fatness in God than by unfailing praise?

Hosea speaks with special emphasis when he says -

> *"Take with you words and return to the Lord ... render the fruit of (your) lips ... (For the Lord says), `I will be as the dew to Israel; he shall blossom as the lily, he shall strike root as the poplar; his roots shall spread out; his beauty shall be like the olive; and his fragrance like Lebanon. They shall return and dwell beneath my shadow, they shall flourish as a garden; they shall blossom as the vine' ... " (14:2-7).*

The prophet portrays God as giving a marvellous promise to Israel, a promise of security, prosperity, wealth, the fulfilment of every aspiration of the people. But the promise is conditional upon the people "*returning to the Lord ... and ... taking with them words*", and rendering to God a sacrifice of praise, the "*fruit of their lips*".

"*Take with you words,*" he said. A remarkable phrase! And one that highlights the importance of guarding our tongues when we are in the presence of the Lord (which is always).

We all need to remind ourselves constantly that "*there is life and death in the power of the tongue.*" No one can escape the effects of the words he speaks. By saying the right things you will obtain the blessing of God. By saying the wrong thing you will lose it. But you can hardly ever go wrong by praising God. You have been destined by God to be his child through Christ, "*to the praise of his glorious grace*" (Ep 1:5-6).

Praise is therefore your most natural spiritual occupation. By praising God in all circumstances you are fulfilling the work of his grace in your soul, you are displaying the attributes of true "*sonship*" and of true faith.

The promise given by Hosea, however, cannot be restricted to physical benefits. If praise does bring natural increase, then far more importantly, for those who take with them right words when they worship God ...

(2) THERE WILL BE SPIRITUAL INCREASE

All that Hosea and other prophets say about the material blessings of God that follow praise must be extended to include spiritual healing and abundance-

> *"I will heal their faithlessness; I will love them freely, for my anger has turned from them" (Ho 14:4).*

It is indeed true that "*the people who know the joyful sound*", and who

> *"rejoice in the name of the Lord all the day", will "walk, O Lord, in the light of thy countenance ... and in thy righteousness shall they be exalted" (Ps 89:15-16. AV).*

Perhaps the most illuminating passage is this -

> *"Day by day they attended the temple together ... praising God and having favour with the people. And the Lord added to their number day by day those who were being saved" (Ac 2:46-47); see also Lu 24:52-53).*

Here is a church in revival. It is growing rapidly. It is held in favour by the people (although it is feared by the government). "*Day by day*" the Lord is adding to its number. What is its secret? No doubt many things; but one is outstanding: "*day by day ...they were praising God!*"

There is an unmistakable connection between the "*day by day*" of their praise and the "*day by day*" of their growth! Without the one there would not have been the other. Luke adds, "*With great joy they were continually ... blessing God.*" Continual praise, continual growth. The people of God lose their increase when praise falls silent. They begin to sin when they stop rejoicing.

Whenever there has been spiritual renewal there has been a revival of praise. Vibrant praise and vigorous spiritual life are inseparable in the economy of God.

BECAUSE PRAISE IS FITTING FOR THE UPRIGHT

> *"Rejoice in the Lord, O you righteous! Praise befits the upright! (Ps. 33:1).*

I have left this until last because it is the chief reason for praise. We should praise God simply because it is right to do so. He is our God, we are his people, and he merits all the worship and adoration we can give him. He should be praised in prosperity and adversity, in pleasure and pain, in good times and evil, in life and in death. He should be praised not merely for what he does, but far more importantly for what he is. So long as there is breath in our lungs our voice should be a voice of praise (Ps 150:6; 104:33).

It may be true, as I have written above, that praise is a key that opens the door to marvellous riches of divine grace. It may be true that praise releases the miracle-working power of God. But even if it were not, even if God has seemingly failed to honour his promise, even if his ways seem capricious and unjust, even if he appears to have forgotten you altogether, he should still be praised.

The most arresting example of this principle is found in the prophecy of Habakkuk. The prophet was deeply troubled by the apparent failure of God to see that justice prevailed, or to help his people. It appeared to him that evil men waxed ever stronger, while God cared nothing for the cruelty and rapacity that were being inflicted on the poor and the helpless -

> *"O Lord, how long shall I cry for help, and thou wilt not hear? Or cry to thee, `Violence!' and thou wilt not save?" (1:2).*

Habakkuk complained bitterly about the perplexities of life, and he demanded to know why God maintained silence in the face of the desperate need of so many innocent people (vs. 12-17).

He decided to hold a prayer vigil on the city wall, and to wait for an answer from God (2:1). The Lord spoke to him. The Lord told him that judgment would inevitably fall upon the wicked (2:6-17). The time of judgment is known only to God, but it is sure nonetheless: "*If it seems slow, wait for it; it will surely come, it will not delay*" (vs. 2-3). In other words, God really is in control, and in due course it will be seen that he has accomplished his will among all nations.

This message offered some comfort to Habakkuk, but he was still not fully satisfied until God spoke the famous words: "*Behold, he whose soul is not upright in him shall fail, but the righteous shall live by his faith*" (2:4; cp. Ro 1:17; Ga 3:11; He 10:38- 39).

This was a demand for uncluttered faith. "*Simply trust me*" said God. No matter how bleak the appearance of life may be, nor how much it may seem that God favours one above another, or that God has failed to honour his promise, we are still required to believe in his unfailing goodness and mercy. He allows no room for doubt. He demands constant faith.

Habakkuk understood. He stilled his complaint. He said: "*The Lord is in his holy temple; let all the earth keep silence before him*" (vs.20). He resolved to wait quietly for the day when God would vindicate divine justice, when evil would be destroyed and righteousness prevail across the earth (3:16b, and vs. 1-15).

Then he gave one of the most thrilling descriptions in the entire Bible of deep trust in the Lord (vs. 17-19). He put himself in the place of a farmer who had faced a series of shattering disasters. This man had once enjoyed a rich and fertile farm. He had been prosperous and wealthy. He had owned orchards, vineyards, fields, sheep, cattle. God had abundantly blessed him.

Suddenly tragedy struck. Pestilence, blight, drought, disease, ravaged his trees, his animals, his crops. His fig trees failed to blossom; there was no fruit on his vines; his olives were shrivelled and parched; his corn, wheat, barley, were blackened husks; his flocks and herds sickened and died; everywhere he looked there was nothing but death. His once green and lovely fields became ugly, his lands were seared, his wealth had withered like a tender leaf on a burning summer day.

Impoverished, devastated, ruined - what should he do? Rail against heaven's malice? Angrily demand an answer from God for failing to help him? There are many fair weather believers who would curse God if such misery had overwhelmed them. But Habakkuk had been given a revelation of the true nature of faith. He knew what he should do. Nor was it a matter of mere duty. His soul in fact delighted to glorify the Lord, and with jubilation he sang -

"Though the fig trees do not blossom,
nor fruit be on the vines,
The produce of the olive fails,
and the fields yield no food,
The flocks be cut off from the fold,
and there be no herd in the stalls,
Yet I will rejoice in the Lord,
I will joy in the God of my salvation.
God, the Lord, is my strength" (3:17-19).

To be able to exult before the Lord in the face of seeming divine failure; to praise God for his own sake, even when there appears to be no hope of reward, nor any possible benefit to be gained from praise - that is the perihelion of faith.

BIBLIOGRAPHY

Ever Increasing Faith; by Smith Wigglesworth; Gospel Publishing House; Springfield, Missouri, USA. 1924.

Law of Faith, The; by Norman Grubb; Lutterworth Press; London,1955.

Master Key Of Faith, The; by Gordon Cove; Coulton and Co. Printers; Nelson, England.

New Creation Realities; by E. W. Kenyon; Kenyon's Gospel Publishing Society; USA, 1964.

Think And Grow Rich; by Napoleon Hill; Fawcett Publications Inc., Greenwich, Conn.1961.

Two Kinds Of Faith, The; by E. W. Kenyon; Kenyon's Gospel Publishing Society; USA, 1942.

Two Kinds Of Righteousness; By E. W. Kenyon; Kenyon's Gospel Publishing Society, USA 1965.

Wonderful Name Of Jesus, The; by E. W. Kenyon; Kenyon's Gospel Pub. Co., USA, 1927.

Yes I Am; by Norman Grubb; Christian Literature Crusade; Fort Washington, Pennsylvania, 1982.

Other Books By Ken & Alison Chant

Angelology
A study of the splendours of the heavenly realm

Attributes of Splendour
Reflections on the nature, being, and glory of God

Authenticity and Authority of the Bible
The Authenticity and Authority of scripture

Better than Revival
A Pragmatic look at Christian Ministry and the Idea of Revival

Building the Church God Wants
Not goal-setting, nor statistics, but faithfulness

Cameos of Christ
OT prophecies fulfilled in the life of Jesus

Christian Life
A positive and creative approach to life.

Clothed with Power
A Pentecostal Theology of Holy Spirit baptism.

Corinthians
Studies in 1 Corinthians

Dazzling Secrets
For Despondent Saints the causes and the cure of depression.

Demonology
Understanding and overcoming our dark enemy

Discovery
Learning and living the will of God

Dynamic Christian Foundations
Studies in Foundational Christian Truths

Emmanuel 1
Jesus: Son of Man.

Emmanuel 2
Jesus: Man who is God.

Equipped To Serve
Understanding, receiving, & using the charismata to Serve

Faith Dynamics
The limitless power of faith in God

Great Words of the Gospel
The major themes of salvation and holiness.

Healing in the New Testament
The healing covenant now.

Healing in the Old Testament
The healing covenant then.

Highly Exalted
The ascension and heavenly ministry of Christ

Mountain Movers
Secrets of mountain-moving prayer

Royal Priesthood
The priesthood of all believers.

Songs to Live By
Studies in the Psalms and Christian worship.

Strong Reasons
The Bible & Science, and the Proofs of God.

The Cross and the Crown
The passion and resurrection of Christ.

The Pentecostal Pulpit
The art of preaching in the power of the Holy Spirit.

The World's Greatest Story
The dramatic first millennium of church history

Throne Rights
Our position and spiritual authority in Christ.

Understanding Your Bible
Studies in biblical hermeneutics.

Unsung Heroines
Sage counsel for women in leadership in the church.

Walking in the Spirit
The Apostle Paul's key to successful Christian living.

When the Trumpet Sounds
Studies in the Return of Christ.